EDITORS
PAUL NASH
DENISE LA NEVE
DAVID MESSINEO
SUSANNA RICH
JOHN J. TRAUSE

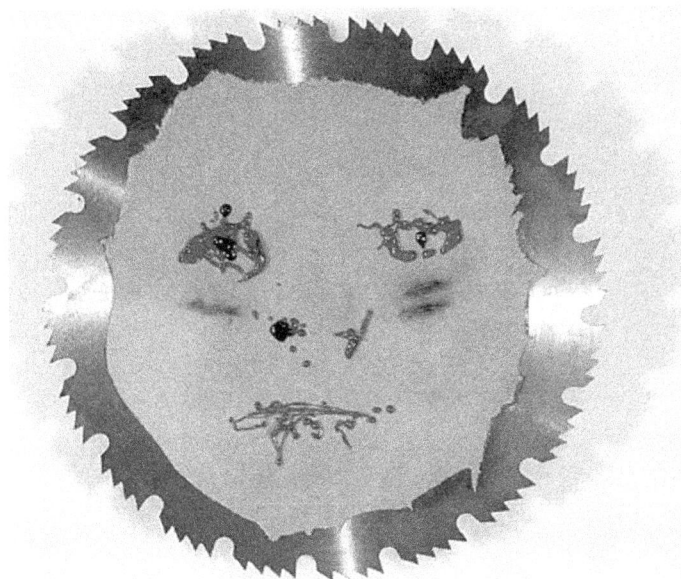

BEYOND THE RIFT:
POETS OF THE PALISADES

THE POET' S PRESS
Pittsburgh, PA

This is the 185th publication of
THE POET'S PRESS
2209 Murray Avenue #3
Pittsburgh, PA 15217

Also available as a PDF E-Book

To order:
The Poet's Press
www.poetspress.org
ISBN 0-922558-44-2 (paperback)
ISBN 0-922558-45-0 (hardcover)

CONTENTS

OF THE ARTS

IN TRANSITION

AGAINST HISTORY

BETWEEN US

ABOUT THE POETS & ARTISTS   149
CITATIONS   165
ART CREDITS   167

FOREWORD

TWO HUNDRED MILLION YEARS AGO, as dinosaurs were poised to become the dominant life forms on earth, a huge pulse of magma welled up from deep beneath the crust, rifting apart the northern expanse of the great supercontinent Pangaea, forming a series of massive rift valleys and eventually the Atlantic Ocean. As North America began to separate from Africa, successive basalt sills created the spectacular 900-foot-high Palisades, as well as Orange, Preakness and Hook Mountains — collectively New Jersey's 'Watchung Mountains.' These igneous sills were all elements of the four-million-square-mile "Central Atlantic Magmatic Province," or CAMP, comprising the largest known upwelling of continental flood basalts in the history of the planet. A mass extinction took place at this time, and some scientists believe the colossal rift event was the culprit, wiping out 40% of all life, paving the way for the rise of the saurians. Continents were on the march. New Jersey, say goodbye to Morocco ...

Nothing of much consequence happened on North America's Atlantic Coastal Plain for quite a while. Then, in the 1990s, disparate elements of the northern New Jersey poetry scene began to coalesce into what some have called the "Palisades Poetry Movement." Already, readings were being sponsored by *The Paterson Literary Review, Sensations Magazine,* and at venues across the Hudson River in New York City. By the middle of the decade, various new poetry series were in full swing in northeastern New Jersey. Among them were popular readings at bookstores in Paramus and in Wayne, plus other new poetry series in Edgewater, Newark, Teaneck, Rutherford, Ridgewood, and Montclair. In 1996, Alda Xavier created a guild called The Rift Arts Forum, which began to host poetry readings and special events, and to put out a literary magazine called *The Rift Arts Forum Publication,* aka *'The Rift.'* Some of the *Rift*-sponsored series and events initiated by Ms. Xavier included: *The Dead Poets Revival,* in Paramus, comparing the work and lives of two famous historical poets each month; *A Drop of Wisdom,* in Englewood, consisting of monthly workshops by individual contemporary poets; *A Special Evening at the Hudson Grill* in NYC in 1998, showcasing musicians, poets and other performers; two themed exhibitions by multiple artists in Jersey City, called *'Flash'* and *'Kites';* the *'Sanctum'* reading series at CBGB's Gallery in NYC in 2001;

< 9 >

staged performances of original plays in North Bergen co-written by 'The Rifters;' and the monthly *North Jersey Literary Series (NJLS)*, which is still ongoing.

Thirty-nine distinguished poets appear in these pages — all have been featured at one time or another in the *North Jersey Literary Series*. This longstanding spoken word and music series began at Marc's Cheesecake in Englewood in 1997, afterward residing for a time at Café Local in Englewood, followed briefly by a stint at Blend Café in Rutherford, then Il Trapezio Café in Nutley, finally settling at Classic Quiche Café in Teaneck. One of our poets is a recent Emmy nominee, another has won the Jefferson Award for Public Service, and four are Pushcart Prize nominees. Seven have produced literary magazines, nineteen have published poetry collections, five are playwrights, and twenty have hosted literary series. Among them are teachers, journalists, scientists, librarians, actors, exhibited artists and musicians, and some of them wear several of these 'hats.'

Poems for this collection were submitted exclusively by past features at *NJLS*, and were selected and organized into six thematic sections by five editors: John J. Trause, Susanna Rich, David Messineo, Denise La Neve and Paul Nash. Mr. Nash provided further editing services. Jamie McNeely Quirk proofread the sections and the individual bios. All work on this anthology was done by members of the poetic community.

Paul Nash

< 10 >

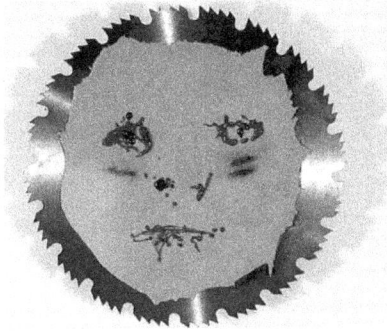

WITHOUT BORDERS

Mullican Pines

Whirring cicadas mimic
the distant doppler whirring
of a lone prop plane

as high summer air shimmers
over the sloping meadow,
down to river's edge.

The Mullica lies shadowed
beneath a cool canopy
of pines and cedars,

a mere trickle caressing
hawthorn, alder, swamp laurel
and wild blueberries.

Its current is like a snake
slithering through flickering,
verdant galleries—

serpentine undulations
gliding quickly out of sight
in bend after bend

as its course slowly widens,
still meandering sharply
through dappled sunlight.

Curves unfold to open marsh
of pink and white Nymphaea
and yellow Nuphar;

cobalt and teal damselflies
dart over a flexed ribbon
of sunsurface sheen.

The river's flow pendulates
over deep pools and winds down
as time slows to smoke.

Along a silken shoreline,
Drosera's tendrils glisten
with bright solar hues —

sequins of blue and lilac
luring wingèd messengers
to Medusa's lair.

A pitcher plant's red-veined leaves
above beds of sphagnum moss
are rainwater cisterns

gleaming in the late day sun,
chalices of buzzing death
for unwary flies.

Night falls softly to ripple
the moon's silver reflection
over secret springs.

Whippoorwills chorus their cries
into atonal vespers
of shrill dementia,

calls rising, then falling off,
jeering nocturnal muses,
presaging the dawn.

Paul Nash and Denise La Neve

< 13 >

The Crows of Teaneck, New Jersey

A familiar sound, like birds but distant,
you leave it alone, but it comes in through
the shut window and causes your waking,
becomes your waking. You say *it is the crows*,
just the crows, but the sound resists,
stands on its own without your memory
and becomes only the breathing
of a motor, an ordinary motor
and not birds at all. You're not even
in that house, it's gone from you, gone
with their death. Before their death
the casement windows bowed outward
and breathed in the sound of crows, dark
consonants before the eyes opened,
and after their death there were crows dying,
even before that summer, up on the corner
one crow lay flattened, swept against the curb
with that fearful loosening of feathers.

Doris Umbers

< 15 >

Early Autumn, Montclair

after Inness

The purpose of the painter is simply to reproduce in other minds the
impression which a scene made upon him. A work of art does not appeal to
the intellect. It does not appeal to the moral sense. Its aim is not to instruct,
not to edify, but to awaken an emotion. —George Inness

Late afternoon, and the great sky
has bubbled into a frenzy of color
and cloud huddled above the graying barn.
I imagine George Inness, peering
maybe through his backyard window,
brushes poised as a storm about to pour
across a canvas. Within the frame
his eye scans landscape from deep shade
to warm light, the rolling depth
of farm field, forceful strokes
laying oil down in direct caress.
The apple tree, the wooden blur of oaks.
A certain shift of space, wide stretch of sight.
Not the russet hues of coolness
and burning browns, but the last grass
still green as ripe lime peel
sprawled over earth, the slow buzz
of autumn creeping quiet through Montclair,
harvest, and the rich scent
of new rain rushing on as quick as youth.

John Chorazy

< 16 >

On the Cape of New Jersey

The fog lifts over tree tops
adorning the hem of the sky
with cornices and crenellations.

Clouds unfist their gauzy breath and
splinters of mist settle over the lowlands.
The buckwheat and hollyhocks stop
to consider
their
fading . . .

to ephemeral dust every night.

This town, this
slumbering wharf,
time-worn by decades of
unlocked doors,
sits on the crest
of a wisp of time,
keeping track of the sunsets
and coaxing the ships
to the shore.

And the sky, stippled with night signs,
turns over and sighs
branch over branch,
like naked brown legs
shifting in their meditations
along the horizon —
a deep crimson blood spill
of lush flesh and faded lace
kissing us
with quivering lips.

Catherine Cimillo Cavallone

< 17 >

Amtraked

. . . there isn't a train I wouldn't take, no matter
where it's going

Edna St. Vincent Millay

Late locomotive negotiates Horseshoe Curve
chugging toward Pittsburgh. Curled in a blanket,
I peer through sleeping-car windows

witnessing militant snowflakes — conquer a stunned earth,
iron-grip branches of terrorized trees —
iced hostages lined up, seized in winter's cold war.

Marigold sun sneaks through breaks of gray,
glazes starched crystals, spent ammunition
in the brutal season's bloodless battle.

An abandoned farm, once born a happy offspring
of the land, dead in bankruptcy ruins; silver coaches
turtle past sheepless meadows into forests,

determined to deliver passengers — weary-of-the-white
to imprisonment in treadmill cities. Frozen in train-time,
packing the diner, an eclectic assembly of worn souls

cajoles: drinking coffee, tea, pop and whiskey.
Addictive strangers who become lovers for a while,
soon to leave each other, most likely forever.

Rusted steel holds the swaying serpent upright,
it crawls years behind schedule, unapologetic
to clock-watching relatives pacing grimy stations.

Some unforgiving voyagers rail against the railroad,
others lavishly toast this creature of emancipation
offering such picturesque parole.

Davidson Garrett

< 18 >

In Moloney's Front Field

for Joan

High on a hillock
in Moloney's Front Field,
in Farrihy, Limerick,
it stands iconic. And open,
it waits unbending
against the low horizon:
a living lunette suspended
yet without leaves.

In the dying light, the night
I see it after so long — dumbstruck —
as if meeting it for the first time.
The sun's last rays caught
in the latticework of a spider's web
and so am I.

At the base rocks half-cover
exposed roots — the movements
and machinations of earlier generations.
Grass grows long and wild, ever widening.
Piss-a-beds and bluebells share
lazy legroom in the dirt.

Moss climbs lichen-like
on two ancient trunks
that twine and hold up this tree
like the bloodlines and branches
of this Irish family — the living
and the gone.

< 19 >

What appears dead this late
April, already at its ends
shows signs of greening
once again.

Patrick Hammer, Jr.

< 20 >

García's House

for Gabriel García Márquez

Thank you for inviting me to your house.
From the outside this stone hut seems so small,
Not much more than a window and a door;
But when I enter I find myself
In rooms opening into other rooms,
Each more astonishing than the last,
With exotic hangings and fantastic clutter
Immaculately arranged.
Like no one else, you turn abundance into clarity.

Thank you for inviting me to sit on this bench
And share this artichoke.
As the story unfolds, the thing comes apart,
Leaf by leaf,
Until, at last, we reach the heart.

There is a warp in the wood of this bench,
And the tiny houses were evenly arranged
So that no one house would get more sunlight
Than any other house,
And they would not belong to the land
Until they had buried one of their own
Like a memory,
Like the memory of the morning
When his father took him to discover ice.

Thank you for walking with me in the garden
Where grapes are the size of lemons
And lemons the size of grapefruits
And blood oranges are everywhere
Telling their tales of love and despair.

Raphael Badagliacca

< 21 >

Song of Casanova

I am Jacques Casanova, Chevalier
de Seingalt, Knight of the Golden Spur,
and I tell of my lineage:
. . . but why bother?
My friends, of course, are much renowned:
I was received, of late,
by Madame de Pompadour,
have spent days on end
with the illustrious Voltaire,
and have stood tall
in the company of popes
and of kings.

Besides, in necessary conditions,
I can lie better than
most can tell the truth
(for I am, above all, *uno literato*).
Yet truth is the only God
I have adored.
Those not truthful to themselves
are not worthy of a life:
their love is lacking.

Fear and hatred kill
the unhappy wretch
who delights in nursing them
in his bosom. It keeps him
in professions of persecution
and moralization.

I am fearless, fulfilled,
full with love,
and a man of letters.
Though letters may lie,
the body, this body,
speaks true.

< 22 >

I have entered,
O, I have pushed my way
into the highest societies.
I have tried — I contrived,
Controlled — and I knew
they would lose their heads
(as I lost mine
more than once),
so I proceed — *io vengo*,
I come.
You open the door
you didn't know you had,
and in I come.

I would be the unseen seed
of the Holy Ghost
to your Blessed Mary Ever Virgin,
if only . . . if only . . .

These are times of Enlightenment,
of immediacy and reason,
here in the boudoirs, and now,
             right now!
But if you blush in your blue veil,
             Venere pudica,
then I approach you from behind,
the *Palio* pounding in the street,
shouting, stampeding, the dust and the dust!
We watch on the crowded balcony
where nobody sees; I raise voluminous
fabrics and I plug you with ease — thus!

< 23 >

from behind,
slowly and quietly
from behind.
We bump in the midst of society —
like bees in your garden,
like winter to spring.
Futile! the many wigs and powders
and laced-up bodices
and floor-length folds
they put between us,
I drum.
And you, O you contain yourself
beautifully, *cara*,
my secret shaft, your soft
rump round.

But I remind you, I am a literary man.
Now a shriveled prick of a librarian
at Dux, *provincia di barbaro*!
I love my books . . . fucking . . . books!
The duke doesn't mind.
I . . . make my way as I can.

And I write:
O Venezia!
Crystal clear city,
my city,
you foggy fragrant mist.
You bulbous humped
whore of snaking glitter.
O you stink, o fragrant lover!
You imprison me,
you rape me;
I raped you.

< 24 >

I reaped the flower and, yellow-thighed,
sighed through the night.

This is my ground,
my watery ground,
my view on the *Histoire de ma vie*!
I struggle in your tight alleys
between your tight thighs —
Non me n'importa — dammela!
Give it, just give it!
And I will return it
four-fold.

I am your erect domes —
your hidden bones
in your darkest hole —
the living *cappela d'ossa.*
I am your San Marco to the moon — Byzantine
and somewhat berserk.
Your *barca* — your *barca* in the canal flowing,
I am your *campanile, lungo,*
your grand cock, till dawn crowing.
I am the hopeful inhale
to your Bridge of Sighs.
And yes! I complete you:
fire to dry your dampness —
water to hiss my fire —
steam-driven pistons,
machine of desire.

< 25 >

I know what you want
and I am what you want.
Sono . . . desiderio.
Sono il tuo desiderio.

My wit, my sharp rapier wit
cuts clean the heads
of the *ancien régime.*
Daughters, wives, moneyed crones
fall prey to this sword,
respirating hard, then soft, then hard
then softly sliding the nape
of her neck;
I have my eternal way,
she her way
to eternity.

Do they want it?
I mesmerize.
When do they want it?
I astrologize.
How do they want it?
I show them how they want it.
Cosi, cosi . . . fottan' tutti.

Your winding stream of fragrance
has led me through this life,
Henriettes, all — your scent
now distilled,
yet opened and bulbous
like cognac in a snifter.

< 26 >

Self-righteously,
you ask if I regret.
I think not . . .

Martir d'amor
non dura che un giorno sol;
Piacer d'amor
dura tutta la vita. . . .

Roy Lucianna

< 27 >

Masquerade

Minstrels and poets are writing checks
as Venice dies,
drowning in a store window
with the canal at her throat
and unbearable pain at sea level.
Her fantasy is bought and sold in every piazza
as tourists seek among vendors
their orient.

Venezia L'otel is open to the masses.
The Doge changes residence
and Pulcinella cries in the arms of Napoli.
The Harlequin dance of the Gondola
is just another expensive ride
or a wind-up toy adorning memories.
San Marco is without question
the name of a pizzeria.

Brighella hangs his head
and the port of Marghera fumes with rage
for those of us who've lived Venice.
Regret bleeds from the slash in our souls
as we sniff her hot August breath;
as Colombina takes her last,
Scaramouche is brought down on his knees.

The Carnevale is over, ladies and gentlemen.
La Serenissima is dead —
her destiny leaves in plastic bags.

Il Carnevale e' finito.
Andate in pace.

Caterina Belvedere

< 28 >

Pedi-Jealousy in the Court

Madame P'ing and Lady P'ong, two lush and blushing lotus buds,
amid the blowing poppies and chrysanthemums,
persimmon trees and peonies, peach blossoms and
cherry inflorescence
                                        luscious lychees
                    jujubes
of the humid hothouse garden hall,
the winding cathouse colonnade,
the great house of the Master's seat,
recline across the jade and ivory table top.

They speak

of old men, fathers, months and mothers, of dogs
        and youths, and brothers
of strength and quarrels, of jaws and household gods,
        of rains and snows, of nephrites and aristocrats,

avoiding talk of little feet, lotus slippers, and plump dumplings,
of on the palm of the hand, on the shoulder, and on the seat
        of a swing,
of within the blankets, within the stirrup, and within the snow,
of below the curtain, below the screen, and below the fence,
the jiggling gait, the jade horse ornaments, the jingle bells upon
        the tiny heels,
of the afternoon the servants heard the Master cry out, naked, spent
        before the slipper closet in the Third Wife's hall,
of the muted mania for cerise silk stitch across pale pink plush,
of the first fumblings in the bath to wash the seed and spittle out.

< 29 >

And then as when a tiny foot shoots soft and slowly through
    the curtains of the boudoir couch
Lady P'ong across their dainty court to Madame P'ing
    pronounces:

"I know that you know that I know that you know that,
although you are Primary Consort and I am only Fifth Wife,
my feet are smaller than yours."

"Hahhhhhh."

John J. Trause

< 30 >

pomegranate

there is a chinese vase
in the outer room

things come back to me in pieces

a phrase, a word

something that she said
so many years ago

pings inside my head
with new meaning

the maiden shows the mandarin
a rare delicacy
slowly unfurled from its purple wrapping

the horses stir, but stay in place
all expression leaves his painted face

before so many jewels
shaped like tears,
red like blood

and then it crashes to the floor
no more a vase

things come back to me
something that she said

the antique carpet near the door
deeply stained
chinese red

Raphael Badagliacca

< 31 >

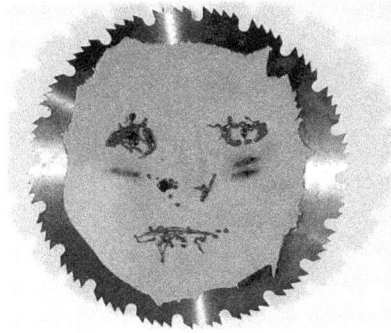

THROUGH TIME

Natural Order

"Eternity is a terrible thought. I mean, when is it all going to end?"
— Tom Stoppard

For John J. Trause

Then self-reflection was invented and
eternity was the first spot on the map.
For many, never ending offered a life's work.

To John, it meant never finding his socks
while neighbors added meaning to their days
and planned for infinite potluck dinners.

John seemed doomed to a lifetime of searching
and banging his head a lot
on the lower, darker corners of his cave.

What would it feel like to wander outside, face up to the sky
feet on grass, feet on sand, feet in water . . . ?
Finding his socks would be such a singular event.
But the hiatus would be unnatural.

Gene Myers

< 35 >

Time

If the earth was still wild,
Filled with heaven's dread . . .
My thoughts linger in that awkward place—
    between blue and red;
I let him take me.

If it was still an untamed world
Free of deadlines and schedules —
Untilled, unacred, unashamed;
I let him — tear me.

If the earth was still wild,
If the elements still struck terror into the hearts
    of priests and prophets
And the High Places still bore that familiar stench
    — the blood of the first-born sons,
I might let him — ravage me.

If it was still that time,
That time before the tyrant time ascended,
Wresting power from imagination,
I might let him — know me.

But everything is too tame now, too clean, too obligatory.
The years will do that
If you let them have their way.

But if the earth was still wild,
If she still courted chaos,
If the air was still thick with myth and legend,
Still drunk on blood and epic,
If the sun still mingled with her early friends —
    here among the Ashtaroth,
I might drink him in
Like fallow ground swallows the monsoons whole
    in their season.

< 36 >

If it was still that time before time snared us,
Dissected our days, hours, minutes, seconds;
That time when time was yet a pauper —
I might let him lay siege to me,
Sack my walls, burn my gates with fire,
Plunder me and lead me away his captive.

Joseph Andrew Sapia

< 37 >

The Idea Future

Stripped down to bare function
Gone is the curlicue
Take away all serifs
Corners square
Learn nothing which does not fit
The immediate eye of the child

Ask a child what it wants to learn
Honey — would you like to know algebra?
I want my cookie!

Tomorrow is clean
Stripped of today's clutter
By virtue of desire
The sunset does not exist —

Come with me now
See Helios gone beyond the darkling mountains
There are a billion colors
And around us are pine needles
And twigs strewn

Feel the wind
Touch the clouds

John Salacan

< 38 >

A Child's Encyclopedia of Quantum Physics

Acausality (a-koz-al´-it-e): n. Phenomenon experienced by small children who get the shit kicked out of them for no particular reason.

Chaos (ka´-os): n. State of mental and/or emotional confusion, the result of having suffered numerous unpredictable beatings at the hands of people you love.

Particular/ways paradox: When this phenomenon was first observed, it seemed completely self-contradictory that the adults you depend on for love and nurture could somehow love you, and at the same time subject you to unspeakable acts of brutality.

Quanta (kwan´ tu): n. [Lat. Neuter of *quantus*] Meaning small child.

Quantum Theory: States that the absorption of a large fist by a quanta, and emission of pleading sobs, is discontinuous of individual units or bundles of energy.

Thermodynamics (ther-mo-di-nam´-iks): [Second General Law of] states that the loss of blood by small noses in a closed system cannot exceed the blood available in said system.

Uncertainty Principle: Maybe he'll kick your ass today, or take you out for ice cream.

Uncle Bob: Distinguished asshole, awarded the "No Balls Prize" for cowardice, twenty years after he first proposed his quantum theory of child rearing, refining it over the course of a decade by repeatedly pummeling and psychologically terrorizing his young nephew. Completely shattering all of his naïve hopes of ever having a safe predictable Newtonian childhood. Ultimately forcing him to abandon his fundamental Cartesian Philosophic presupposition: "*Cogito*

< 39 >

Ergo Sum (I Think Therefore I Am)," and to adopt in its stead a radically new axiom, one that gave a more accurate description of chaotic young reality: "I Am Therefore I Get My Ass Kicked."

Joseph Andrew Sapia

< 40 >

A Simple Current

Between the foxglove and the pearl
a slinky little tendon swirls what seems
a meaningless apparel, toting beams
of dark fluorescence into unkempt world,
wrapping cord in chattel, card in cane
until a scopic fracture wreaks
a darting eye, dissolving face,
and every name unsaid.
                              How can the
pitter-patter spit quite so wetly and
splat so spappily when the afternoon
doorway is empty? Where stands the one
little girl with a handful of licorice?
                              Recant,
tulips — bark, chains — the sated mare
is charging in the rain, mad-eyed
and rare, and if you stare her down you can
be her, foam-flecked, high-toothed,
whirling on the world, rearing
into this deep breath:

Richard Loranger

< 41 >

Along St. Joe's Stream

How do I describe it? How?
How do you describe what's not there?

Does a flower push itself up
Under weighted mantle of air?

Does the sun struggle up its rosy vine?
Does a bird fight the muscled arm of air?

No, they all slip with ease
'Cross the worshipful ether

As smoke from a candle ascends
Through the idea of a mind awakened,

As the limbs rise up with new strong winds
Billowing in the will

And conundrums once impossible
Snap like twigs underfoot.

Such is running — swift, fleet
Oh! Endless ease, so far beyond

The trudge of walking
Seen from swift-furrowed wind.

It brings me among boulders
Behovered by dark hemlock

Brings me like glint flung
Across quick new terrain,

< 42 >

An effort without care
Or envy of soaring starwise,

For the solid earth
Bids my feet fly.

John Salacan

< 43 >

Twenty Thousand Legumes Under the Sea

We once thought that the amount of variability in ocean life from one place to the next was merely infralapsarian. Now we understand that to swap sea horses while crossing the river is a bad idea. From cockatrice to earwig, this kingdom knows how many licks to get to the center of a basilisk. Oh Kissimmee, Okeechobee, we've Hitchiti water.

A pervert will turn someone aside from a right religious belief to a false or erroneous one, usually within an erogenous zone. Few can name the goddess of married love, but doesn't she begin with a F___ and end with A? Don't we all end with a ?

The germination of doubt makes a crepitaculum in the wedded beds of sectarians. Lamarck is coming into his own. Supplant evolution, the infidels are too green to give a fig. A pod of seals, hawing over the hemicotyledons of a haricot.

C.D. Russell

< 44 >

Slipstream

". . . the gods grow old along with the men that made them. But storms sway in heaven, and the god-stuff sways high and angry over our heads . . . Even the gods must be born again."
— D. H. Lawrence, The Plumed Serpent (Quetzalcoatl)

"I am the 'great storm' who goes forth out of the 'great below.' I am the Lord of the Land."
— from the Sumerian creation myth Enki and the World Order, circa 2000 BC

She unfurls the line
and casts it skyward,
toward those watchful eyes in the storm,

plumed serpent eyes
that welcome the clouds of dust,
cartwheeling leaves and stinging sand.

Tethered to a black ring of stone,
the massive kite bucks and rises,
a colossal manta ray rustling
in a turbulent sea of dry air.

Straining block and tackle,
she hoists with callused hands
and climbs the taut halyard,
lost above the mists and the cliff walls.

Now only distant shadow,
the great kite shivers in space
as she grips the time-worn flybar
to adjust outhaul and canvas.

To the west amidst towering cloudbanks
Lord Quetzalcoatl
stares fiercely down at her . . .
she cuts the line

< 45 >

and spirals deliriously
out of control,
riding the slipstream past consciousness
into feathered oblivion.

Soaring soundlessly above ozone,
flocks of famished songbirds
devour her fleeting thoughts

and carry them southward
to winter in Patagonia,
where they are shed like wisps of down.

They seep slowly through earth's stone pages
to an ancient shoreline,
entering the cold, petrified bones
of feathered saurian ancestors,

trespassing without hesitation,
stirring faded memories
into ghostly whispers,

blending those with her own final sigh.

Paul Nash

< 46 >

When Gravity Stops Working

There are days
when you feel
your wings growing in,
long and sleek,
and oiled with promise.

Preen them.
Ruffle them.
Hear them clatter
together.
Then run them
over your breast.
Feel them brush against
your sides, your back.
Let them be a reminder:
there is more to you
than only earth.

These are the days
when you press
your elbows together,
arch your back and feel
the air
cupped and rounded and solid
beneath you.

Your usual gravity
will not suck you down
this day,
won't bruise you
against the carpet.
Leap off
the arm of the couch.

< 47 >

Snap out
your feathers
like geisha's fans
and hang
in the air.

Lean into the glide.
Trust you will come
to your perch and settle
on your own two feet.

Gravity only stops working
when you jump.

Dorothy Alexander

< 48 >

Fallen Bird, Oven

For Sylvia Plath

Days of eyedropper meals,
cotton batting in a cardboard box

& toothpick splints, but you couldn't
stop what gravity ordained

— one smashed wing, one mercy
left   — the only thing, the only

thing you couldn't do
at first, then love came

odorless, soft sleep through
the nostrils, a bit lingering

in you until one anvil of a
morning no

body would argue
with a woman snapped

off at the shoulder.
Had you always let

doors close
behind you.

Just enough breath
to get you through.

Jamie McNeely Quirk

< 49 >

These Upright Fellows

Here they stand
tall as household ladders
after a long season of rain
and bushels of sun

that shines still
on their bony backs
and highlights the gold
of their butter-sweet faces.

Come, all day they will follow
you if you keep in step with them
and avoid the sunless shadows.
Come into the cool of evening

with these upright fellows
who stoop and whisper their secrets
now that they know you after
this long, drenched day.

Their eyes on you, their green lashes
close and invite you to bed
down at their loamy feet
for the night's well-earned hours.

Patrick Hammer, Jr.

< 50 >

Chemistry of Rain

Lightning, thunder, a strong metallic odor —
Sound on the windshield, window, and sidewalk,
On rooftops, street corners, and umbrellas,
The shape of an ovary, oval, or orb,
A capsule the size of a gnat or a sperm.

Each drop takes a unique journey,
Condensed in the air or coalesced in descent,
Some evaporate and some make it down.
Curious eyes see where these drops hit —
Little pinwheels turned by invisible hands,
Tiny records spinning their music—
The ripples flow out from the center.

These rhythms copy the flash of life,
From the spot of origin out to a full body,
To decay and the last breath.
Like time, these wakes turn in an instant,
Each one blinking in and out, split-second neon,
Light switch flicked on and off,
A galaxy here then gone.

They come from a trinity of elements,
Protium, deuterium, tritium, a piece of atom,
The hydrogen present three minutes into creation,
In the heat of many suns, the first life on a planet,
Sentient beings who create and destroy
And return to the clouds once more —
Lightning, thunder, a strong metallic odor.

Thomas D. Jones

< 51 >

April 5, 2006   Fort Greene, Brooklyn

Snowflakes big as feathers fall on Brooklyn by the billions
on this gentle day of April and amazingly
disintegrate upon the tar-encrusted countryside
somehow by this spectacle made earthlike once again.

I am so excited that I tourist all the windows
in this tiny hole of wood in which I catenate my days
and drag the giant chair to watch the snowflakes big as pixies
grace the battered brickscape that I normally ignore.

For a magic hour I am mercifully taken
to a world without corruption as the snowflakes big as ashes
drifting by the billions cleanse this lunatorium
we call a governed culture and I hope it's snow.

Richard Loranger

< 52 >

Like   Dust
. . . like dust

Like powder
       soft
  like quiet
      still
  like faint
      blue arrives.

Like haze
      white
  like light
      beams
  like dust settles
      we lie.

As morning resurrects
  and stone breaks,
    birth began with warmth —
      it grew with love,
        flowered with time
          and passed like pollen
              like dust.

As night envelopes and clouds obscure,
  memories haunt
    luminescent
and whispers' allure,
  like wind they rustle,
    arousing the creatures to bustle.

< 53 >

Deep as hunger,
  wide-so-eyed,
    thirsty with lustful intent;
      courting for sport,
        bleeding the prize,
          like water, emotions are spent.

Now rich in our wealth
  and full with ourselves,
    we'll promenade at the cusp,
      for now is the time
        in the past to reside

        like white
          like powder
            like dust . . .

                                    Peter Jaworowski

< 54 >

OF THE ARTS

Eugene Turk

Like an Ingmar Bergman movie there's a momentary
silence, cirrus in a frozen distance, and somewhere
an old dog shudders, tethered to a pole.
My father used to say a barking dog at night meant

someone near was going to die, and he was often right,
but I don't remember hearing howls before his passing.
Today December greets me childlike,
wraps frigid hands around my legs — it's been at play

all night and comes inside to warm itself on me.
I learned about a friend long unheard from, heard
the story of his death and how he said
"it's beautiful" before he went

and I am sickened by the irony of grief.
I have a picture of him speaking verses, the photo
black and white, like us, and he is dark and large beside me.
We were drinking at a party in the Village, talked

about New Orleans, some verses of Bob Dylan.
So much for poems, so much for smoke and wine, now gone.
Once, inside a dream, I saw the shoreline of a lake
I used to visit with my family. I don't recall

the water, not the sky, and not a single face,
only the shoreline. I think it's meant to be this way.
We see just the outside edges before we learn
the courage to wade in.

John Chorazy

< 57 >

Curves

Today at the beach I am aware
of curves. Past the waves,
behind the sheen of silver or ice
where sky sags into sea, the horizon
is a curve drawn in intense blue.
So is the visor on the fisherman's cap
shading the curve of his face.
Each time he flings the line,
it arches through the air, then sinks.
He holds the rod tight and waits,
dozing in the sun. Then,
feeling a tug, he grows alert.
Slowly he reels the fish in.
It leaps high above the water,
wriggling and twitching,
falling from curve into curve,
trying to rip the pain from its mouth.
Even on shore, the fish
does not stop thrashing;
it makes a deep bed in the sand
as if to escape through the earth.
The fisherman removes the hook
and tosses the fish
into a bucket with water
where it leaps almost to the rim.
It is drowning on air. Curved
around panic, its mouth is open,
the tiny teeth useless
as are the fins that have forgotten
how to fly. All afternoon,
as the fish begs for its life
behind the man's back, I glance
at the bucket handle —
a curve waiting to be picked up.
Not even a whimper
from the fish — all I hear is

< 58 >

thumps against metal,
water sloshing from side to side,
and the wind that keeps moaning
in my ears long afterwards,
even as I sleep.

Marianne Poloskey

< 59 >

Misericordia

Michelangelo's Pietà

"I merely uncover what God has already placed inside the stone."
Michelangelo Buonarroti

This rock, this stone,
white pure
like her love, like her son
in her hands, in my hands,
empty and wanting —
his soul reborn inside the stone,
this mass to be form, to be shape.
Inside my head I see his face.
This rock, this stone,
it is heavy
like a mountain on my chest,
a Madonna, it is pain,
like a spear in my side.
In his side
I split the veins
hidden in the rock,
and I chisel the veins
that bulge in his neck.
Then I hammer his back
like my heart that pounds,
and pound on his chest,
and form his hands
with hands that bleed,
and I curse this rock
as they cursed my lord.
Now I smooth my sins
like wounds he healed
and I cleanse his feet —
He cleansed our sins.
Inside the rock, my death,
there's a canyon of stone

< 60 >

on the folds of her dress,
and I carve his soul inside the rock
and breathe his life inside the stone,
and pound and chisel and carve and cut
his hands, her hands, my blood, my bones.
In the rock, in the stone,
I die his death a thousand times
and birth divinity white as hope.

Caterina Belvedere

< 61 >

Nun Flying Through Walls

After Míklós Melocco's sculpture, Budapest

Ancient corner convent door opens to
a newsstand — Fuji disposables; paprika, like
red horns, dangling; holographic Jesus over the Danube.
Even locals rarely know the stone woman above

who flies horizontal through the corner —
soles, black shoes, furls of blue habit
are a stone kite on Judge Petermann Street;
belt to granite wimple — she bursts into Townhouse Road.

Wall angles to wall where a magician might slice
through a woman all plumes, décolletage, net tights.
Here, the pink stucco corner chevrons out from her belly.
Bus stop bench across from her, I sit with the lover

to whom my father shuttled on Delta — United
States to Hungary, future to past. My red tulips
wilt in her lap. We look at the nun. I ask how
one manages decades of longing for the Beloved.

She tells me the only freedom is to turn back,
like Lot's wife, until you become the pain.
Here she looks at me. I make myself still.
"Only stone can pass through stone," she says.

We look up, again. "Yes," I say, "Let no one
know whether the hands at your lips
pray, hide secrets, or protect your joy."
"Or," she adds, "stop hunger with silence."

Susanna Rich

< 62 >

The King of Ragtime

St. Louis, Missouri, 1899

'Honest John' Turpin,
his brother Tom, Louis Chauvin . . .
They all dere at the Silver Dollar Saloon
huddled round de corner table
thick as thieves.
A fancy dan slips in through
'the family entrance'
and Madame sends a girl over.
We have company now, and need a professor.
Seven high. Deuce low.
Mr. Joplin hand hold a tiger
so he fold, and gits up to git down
ticklin' the ole eighty-eight.
Down-up. Down-up.
Bass chuggin' like a piston
set the floorboards a-buzzin'
an' de john's feet to tappin'
whilst de melody flirts wid de beat —
rushin' fowad, layin' back,
rushin' fowad, layin' back —
dart like a mayfly on de river,
firs' dis way 'n' dat.
Chippie raise her skirt jess above her knee
an' dance the hootchie-kootchie.
Sport be chucklin' to hisself,
This sho ain't no cotillion cakewalk!
Now Mr. Joplin, he a cut above
de rest o' dem honky-tonk professors
at Mother Johnson cuttin' contests acrosst de street.
He'll shoot out a two-step or lay down
the sixteens with a zig-zaggin' jag
picked on a jig piano
that'll put dem other march kings to shame.
Still 'n' all it ain't no picnic.

< 63 >

A man gotta win his bread somehow.
He got no truck wid
coonjinin' roustabouts at de levee camp
moanin' the blues.
No party t' de hokum
of the minstrel shows.
Mr. Scott Joplin a gentleman.
He gonna write a opera.
He the king!
Everybody know
he write *The Maple Leaf Rag.*

Brant Lyon

< 64 >

John Coltrane

There is no instrument like a man,
churches burning in his blood,
their smoke too heavy to rise up
and out of him, too heavy with
blackness. There is no instrument
like a man in the house his parents
left him, its empty rooms and
empty clothes and the sunlight
bouncing off a cracked teapot
no longer strong. There is no
instrument like a man walking
on the edge of the street with
one foot on the curb and one foot
in the gutter somewhere between
heaven and hell without weight
or wings. There is no instrument
like a man with his father's hands
building things on air too light
to stay together, sculptures
on a mountain top made out of
dirt and dust, most beautiful in
the last seconds before they
change, before they break and
scatter and fly.

Josh Humphrey

< 65 >

Fin de Siècle

i.

Spoon River Anthology

Clearly we are Midwesterners,
same small-towners, all
talking that flat corn language.

Yet all our talking does not
bring us together.
We do not speak a shared identity,

but rather our separation
from each other, from the town,
from ourselves.

Each alone, each alien,
each beyond death
in individual graves,

no one to nod and
encourage us to say
what happens next.

And yet we do go on,
speaking just to speak,
telling no one everything,

dreaming on into the dark
and inhospitable universe,
a small, disappointed voice

full of regrets and remorse,
a blighted consciousness
acutely aware of its blight,

< 66 >

the voices of the dead
who were dead a long time
before we died.

Stumbling around posthumous,
stunned, decaying,
oblivious, petty,

mortal, foolish,
uncomprehending.
Like you.

ii.
The Waste Land

1.

Everything we thought we knew,
for two thousand years,
until a few minutes ago,
was a lie.

It'll take a while to get over that.

2.

What do we have left? Fragments, at best.
Little snippets of meaning,
remembered out of context,
stuck together in collage.

Words sit next to each other
like strangers on the bench of a city park,
related somehow,
yet anonymous and unspeaking.

< 67 >

Lines bounce off each other
randomly, like
billiard balls: some go into
the pocket of the reader's mind,

others reverberate endlessly
from cushion to cushion
until they finally come to rest,
their energy exhausted.

3.

From beneath the ruins
of the European Temple,
desperate voices cry out,
trapped and crushed
under tons of fallen rubble.

We can hear Dante buried
under the remains of Christianity,
calling out in pain
like one of his own damned souls.
And he sounds like us,
his voice curiously modern;
his dark wood is our dark wood.

Ovid manages to wheeze out
scattered pieces of classical tales,
a name whispered here,
a line echoed there,

but there's no time to tell anything
from beginning to end,
the whole thing's been pulled
down around our ears.

< 68 >

4.
And yet here we are still living.

iii.
The Postmodern Carpenter

1.
The Postmodern Carpenter
stares at tools,
dreams what a hammer can do
to a nail

to a wall
to the carpenter's own finger
to somebody's head:

all manner of useful violence,
but the carpenter doesn't want
to be useful.

2.
The carpenter listens to the song
the tools sing
while they wait in their box.

3.
The carpenter builds
a workbench
out of tools.

The carpenter's heart
resembles the tools
it was made from.

< 69 >

4.

The purest hammer
never strikes
a nail.

The purest action
of hammering
needs no hammer,

yet hits the nail
on the head
anyway.

Jonathan Hall

< 70 >

Opera on Opera

Beatrice's Venetian fingers in stately promenade ascended
The upper register of her dressing-room piano.
   The Mediterranean archangel
Who presided over the stage and many rooms
   of the Paris Opera
Sipped from a crystal flute and parted her lips to liberate
   the sonic wine of her throat.

Croak!

In the mirror on the wall on the other side of the instrument
She saw eyes transporting perplexity and fright.
Her right hand, resuming, rested on a simple major chord.

Croak!

In the mirror was a gondolier's daughter who despised
   the canals
And deified Donizetti. The newspapers christened her
   La Merlette,
Blackbird, in honor of her luxurious Italianate tresses.
Were they party to this, they would rename her
   La Grenouille, Frog.
She drained the flute and wiped the nervous excess
   from her chin.
Then, a tentative arpeggio at the keyboard's lower end.

Croak! Croak!

Past the closet full of costumes, behind the jonquil-papered
   walls,
Erik cackled in the gloom. He rolled the empty vial
   in his skeleton palm
And tossed it over his shoulder. His ear pursued the echo
   of shattered glass.
That was either F# or G, he mused.

< 71 >

He pulled off his mask and fingered the absence
    where the rest of humanity
Boasted a nose. Ugliness is the new Catholicism.
Adjusting his cloak, spinning volte-face on his heels,
    he returned
In satisfaction to his well of darkness.

When one is known as the Phantom,
One must live up to the reputation.

Joel Allegretti

< 72 >

Cigarettes, Coffee, and Beer, Oh Dear

For Jackson Pollock

Cigarettes, coffee, and beer, Oh dear,
remain my diet, the drip drip drip
of a rattled hand and magic wand
my staff of life.

And so I drive drive drive
and expedite
with stains and ashes
through storm and strife
until I crash against the canvas
of life

     on the floor

         in a barn

             at the farthest point east

of an island and a state
of death in life   totally totemically

     crushed in the crash

cras   s

ly

John J. Trause

< 73 >

A Denial

For Kurt Cobain, 15 years later[1]

In the darkness of Aberdeen
mills and litter and daughters of mills.

A bridge to live under[2]
a bridge to cross over
graffiti sings to you from the other side.

Your mouth is a wound
through which you suck in knives
that lodge in your entrails and fester
there. Your life is an infection.

Rage out of a hot stomach:
your body rejects your body
like the offered heart
of an accident victim.

You are not a victim.
You are not an accident.
You did not die of your disease.[3]
We did not kill you.

Jonathan Hall

---

[1] Kurt Cobain, founder of Nirvana, was found dead on April 8, 1994.
[2] "Homeless, Cobain slept on friends' couches. At one point, he lived under a bridge in Aberdeen [Washington], an arrangement chronicled in *Nevermind*'s "Something in the Way." (*Rolling Stone*, April 16, 1992).
[3] "He's been suffering from a longstanding and painful stomach condition perhaps an ulcer aggravated by stress and, apparently, his screaming singing style." (*Rolling Stone*, April 16, 1992).

< 74 >

A Series of Paintings by Jimmy Ernst
On the Broken Glass
Of His Mother's Bedroom Window

Jesus in Capernaum, with his foot in a prostitute's hair

Five sullen parabolic peaks
in a cadmium rain,
a large circle like a dead heart —
He studies the top of her head.

Jesus teetering on the Sea of Galilee

Hard rivulets of olive green
on white palette-knife scratches,
anxious hints of canvas,
ancient ripple.

Jesus entering his home town without bothering to unpack

He straightens His robe
with a cluster of delicate strokes.

Jesus, hands on a child

Laughter can be heard on the inside of a house.
Birds are hinted at with sharp edges in the sky.

Jesus in the face of seven devils

He is a Jew, remember.
Yes, there is a gesture,
the subject collides with the frame,
more energy that way,
the dangerous shape
of what surrounds Him.

Donald Zirilli

< 75 >

Five-Year-Old Blind Girl Playing Piano

When you repainted *Starry Night*
you only wanted the *Mars Black*,
to roll it on the sky with five
stars made of masking tape, and asked

that your new art be studied while
Yoo Ye Eun played *Für Elise*, so
I wore my headphones through the stile
and stood before your square zero.

A chord of stars were poking through.
I wondered how you found my cries
in their precise locales, and who
was shining on the other side.

Donald Zirilli

< 76 >

Waldo, Find My Mother

somewhere in my thronging *do-do-do*s days
    — tell me she's hiding, like the one *you* we, no matter, spot
in The Nasty Nasties Castle massed with mummies,
vampires, ghouls; in the toque-jammed Cake Factory
of the frosted and the iced; in the Wild, Wild

West with gallons and gallons of hats, swinging
saloon doors, Conestogas, colts and Colts.
If only she *were* you, Mr. Cartoon Man
    with the Cat-in-the-Hat
Stovepipe — the can without lids — slipped over her body
same lie-down stripes prisoners wore (except black-

and not red-and-white). Might she be behind bards (oops,
haha — bar(d)s) anyhow, meant to ask — *Think she's in jail?*
Sing Sing? She's always on the look out for whomever
she can thieve from — men and me. I'm turning the page,
Waldo, to forests of antlers, bucks (as in money),
    a rummage

of pants and beards, wallets, bald heads. Slipped
    on a stocking cap,
she has, one husband's down vest, the other's belts — let her
whiskers grow. Must've — no mother skirts in here, no
aprons with floury hand prints (prince).
    Where to look next?
Hang at the mall (them all, the maul)? How do we spy

her in a ma(lai)ze of bar(d)codes? She might be sitting
on Old Nick's lap. But where are her posey-pursed lips,
    lines of
penciled brows slipped into carnival face cut-outs
    of Pat Boone,
Pavarotti, George W . . . ? You're right: if my mother were
my mother she'd be a cut-up, not a cut-out. My MO's to look,

< 77 >

look for what can't be found in this Cosmic hide-and-seek
   this Olympiad of perpetual peek-a-boo, peek-a-boo,
peek-a-boo for aught. For all my *boo, boo, boo* —
      all my *so-sad*s,
*she-done-me-wrong*s, ghost conversations —
      where'd you put her?
Are *you* my mother? Emissary of Elusion in Male Drag?

I know, I know — you can't be — *you* live for me to find you.
And I know I will. I know when I have. But nothing
      stays with me
while I'm looking for her — not father, not children,
      not love.
+I'm a wacky moth pummeling a screen — as if,
with enough tapping, I could become the looking
      I do to be.

Even here — I'm creating a something-made to reflect,
      to look out
for, to look to me. Oh, treasure of my life, World of Words,
holding the place of emptiness too horrible to conceive —
find my mother in here. Find my . . . Find me my find me.
Find me my me . . .

                                        Susanna Rich

< 78 >

To My Peter Pan

In which Tinker Bell describes her love.

His hands are like no other hands. One
is like a girl's hand that bends beneath me
with softnesses, a wrist that betrays bone.
The other carries a battle in a pinky scar,
the indentation of a sword hilt hours gone.
I am small for him, and simple. I am jealous
for him, even though I could be as cold
as a mermaid, as beautiful and as calculating
in the parts that lie beneath the dark line
of the sea. I could be as English as a lady trading
kisses and wearing a smile with a pout.
I could be an Indian princess for him to save.
But that is not the part I play. I play the light.
I play the spark that he does not know he needs.
I play the glint on the edge of his dagger that
is always waiting to die for him, to drink down
the poison before it wets his lips. And this
is how I love him. Instead of thinking, I am
the light, instead of desiring anything more.
Instead of sleeping, I move inside my box,
spin so that I glow, just in case some noise
should wake him to the night that is deeper
in Neverland than the inside of your eyes,
that is the only thing he is afraid of. I will be
the thing he sees, a bright heart in the darkness,
where the stories end in mystery, where even
the immortal boys feel their age.

Josh Humphrey

< 79 >

IN TRANSITION

Beyond the Veil

I

A taffeta chrysalis
enshrouds her
in delicate folds
like some fabled Bedouin queen.

A chiffon veil
threaded with gold shimmers above
a robe of black muslin
covered by lambskin cloak.

Her questing hands
remove an ancient puzzle box
of finest-grained mahogany
from beneath shifting ivory sands.

Recalling an Arabian thief's simple words,
her trembling fingers find expression
as interlocking slats are realigned
to reveal a secret cavity.

II

An opalescent pearl lies inside
upon a bed of velvet feathers —
her fevered touch awakens this jewel,
which suddenly bursts into fine powder.

< 83 >

A jinn stands before her, naked,
muscles dormant beneath flesh —
jade eyes pierce her silent mirage,
see her hidden sorrow.

III

A taffeta chrysalis enshrouds her:
a chiffon veil threaded with gold
above a robe of black muslin
covered by lambskin cloak.

He strips each layer away tenderly
till only her exposed cracked visage
stares back with hollowed eyes —
her final mask, herself.

His lips press against plaster mouth,
shattering Sienese clay;
their embrace — a fixed point
in a helical curve of spiraling shards.

Denise La Neve

< 84 >

The Absence of Crows

For my father

The sound of crows and I imagine you
kneeling on the edge of the lawn,
cutting away the stray blades of grass,
your knees sunk into the faded green foam,
which gives beneath like flesh, your back arched
in a kind of silence, except for the crows.

This year, in the absence of crows,
cicadas quicken in the rising heat.
I kneel to watch one emerge wet-winged
from its perfectly round hole under
the roses I cut and bring you
and where the canna erupts, a dark shape
against my new neighbor's boundary.
I touch the earth where it was and remember
the stag beetle fetched from the bottom
of the watering pail, and how I held it
out to you, a perfect specimen,
its whip-like antenna intact —
we laid it on the window sill to dry,
only to find it gone in an hour.

I will not dig up the irises this year.
Enough to have imagined you here again,
except for that moment some bird came
of a sudden, its shadow nearly palpable
in this space beside me.

Doris Umbers

< 85 >

A Day in the Water

I take the plunge into cool water
And shiver as it moves aside
To make room for the shape of my body
Which has traveled long and far,
Many a gannet's journey,

A thousand times the stroke of an oar.
I feel like a canoe floating heavy as iron
Yet light as dust, a speck swimming
In the current of time and space.

The ripples fan out from the center
And double back upon me,
Waves as strong as light
Or the spirit on the wind,
The lick of breath from the sun.

I imagine I am a ship in the void,
A wave particle or neutrino
On the way through interstellar sea
To the past or the future.

Wet and naked, squeezed head first,
I reach the other side and cry
For my lover to wrap me safe
And keep me from ravages of age.

Thomas D. Jones

< 86 >

Empty Vessel

You put your faith
and stock in me,
your hopes and dreams.

I sit like an empty boat.

You fill me
with your valuables —
bags and heaps
of the precious stuff.

I sink quietly to the bottom.

Roy Lucianna

Divine Fire

I lit a light.
So sorry you caught fire,
burning and raging,
transforming and returning to charcoal
like Saint Joan
in her
transformation
to sainthood
from
medium
rare.

Roy Lucianna

< 87 >

Last Portrait of My Father

Content to be driven — your hands
hold nothing steady — you navigate
nonetheless, this first fall drive
after Mother's death.

Your lips wet as though water
escapes everywhere from your body.
Tires shush as we go — Whitehouse,
Somerville, Frenchtown — until we pass

the place where you photographed
her in a field of Queen Anne
and oxeye (the photo that curls now
in the corner of your room). I ask

you to turn, see the sun blaze crimson
in a window across the road,
but you sit stuck in her memory.
Soon October itself would fall away.

And what remains of that day
is not the unrelenting sun,
but you, your last ride, and her
somewhere in the space between us.

Doris Umbers

< 88 >

My Father's Orchard

as seen in 1975

Birds that sang its praise
have vanished one by one.

A creek that sinuously
embraced the land
no longer runs its course.

The fruit trees that remain
bear witness to the glory
of what this fertile land once was:

a dream in one man's heart,
a man who knew no boundaries,
a man who loved these fields
more than his own life.

Father, if you could see
your orchard now,
your tears, like a torrent,
would inundate this land!

Estrella Gabrie-Garcia

< 90 >

And When I Die, I Hope They Say

He noticed small things: a bird's shadow,
a puddle's shrinking circumference,
and the labor of spiders. He breathed between
these shards of daylight as we breathe between
walls, between our comings and goings.

When it rained, he walked with Jesus beneath
a wood's canopy. They listened to the storm's
percussion: drops drumming an awkward
tempo against the smooth backs of maple leaves.
They laughed, spoke of his children, and why he

found his wife in a wildflower's sway. He reclined
in tall grass, letting each blade read his skin's Braille
until night began its slow spiral above him.
When he left, he was content with the air
in his palms — he rarely asked for more.

S. Thomas Summers

< 91 >

At the Edge of the Forest

As we walked
hand-in-hand in the pine forest,
our legs hemming a line in unraveling ferns
(delicate twigs that we were),
our feral spirit mingled
in woodland hues of greens, arbor browns
and the rich crimson pulp of secrets.

I reminisce now over those picnics,
those safe and sacred get-us-away's,
oozing with brie and arugula
and hearty, rustic breads —
fresh, round and washed down with a good Port —
a beating red juice pouring
into our throats, merging with fumes
left behind by our famous kisses.

Love was found. Love was lost.
Should it matter now? Yes, I think it should.
Memory, friend or foe, is after all master.
Like cement, it fills gaps in our cracked
awareness and gives us the complete story.

As a great stand of white pines at Lake Tiorati
towers over my present puny minutes,
and as their cones hold tiny seeds
for the promise of conifers to come,
I rest now and again
in a world at the edge of the forest.

S. Gili Post

< 92 >

7,000 Prayers to a Wolf

I gave 7,000 prayers to a wolf
and I sent him off to find God.

I wrapped my prayers in strips of my own flesh,
so that God, knowing my scent,
would know that they were mine.

I cut out the wolf's tongue
so he could not taste my prayers.

I wrapped his eyes in black cloth and wax,
and bound these about his throat,
so he could not see my prayers.

I clipped his nose
so the scent of my sweet, desperate prayers
would not entice him to stop, and to eat,
along the way.

But bound and blind and voiceless,
unable to sniff his way,
the wolf got lost . . . stumbled . . .
dropped my prayers.

And then, other wolves came along.

And by morning,
all of my prayers
were gone.

George C. Harvilla

< 93 >

Work Study

All dark morning, I crack
brown eggs against the steel
rim of a bowl —

four dozen, a small
army of once-potential
birds now sloshing

in clear, thick soup — those unmade,
broken hearts! Sunny nebulae
swimming, white threads

trail, still flagella. The metal
Gong, Gong like a Buddhist bell
calling the kitchen into focus,

I stand. I'm slowly expelling
my own eggs into cotton, cramping
to lose anything childlike.

In my hands, some eggs split
like their plastic Easter twins,
others crumble, walls

thin as paper, my thumb submerged
in a planet's core,
wrists shrink-wrapped

in albumen, old song in my head,
a scoopful of shells at my feet
I'm used to walking on.

Jamie McNeely Quirk

< 94 >

Misty

There are feelings everywhere —
rolling waves of emotions
crashing against rocks
on a deserted shoreline

where no one sits
to enjoy the warm spray
of all this love, this passion
. . . it is simply water in the air.

There are no flowers either,
only dunes of sand littered
with dry prickly bushes
which no path will ever cross.

The mist is carried away
on currents of wind, rising
to meet the sun where it will
dissipate . . . or become a cloud —

the very cloud that rains today,
whose misty grayness saddens you
because you're missing someone
you've never met, and fear you never will

. . . not a second time anyway.

Eddie Rivera

< 95 >

Sick-Eyed

Muzzle my jaw, my beastly voice,
and make speech cease . . .
cease the drumming, the incessant pounding
of soundless mutterings
bringing my attention out
into the middle of the floor — dragging me on a leash.

A procession of throbs,
marching galloping throbs,
bakes my brain in a kiln of industrial aches
and stained-glass voices.
No room for *Hemicrania*[1], time's saboteur,
but for silence and black potent darkness.

Radioactive tears ooze publicly,
while notes too beautiful to bear
wash my temple with a chorus of mutating mutes,
keeping rhythm to my tip-toeing
away to safety.
Lonely as a bat hanging in a cave,
I feast on a diet of no light, warm veins — no admirers.

Rubicon, Rubicon:
what treacherous stream are we crossing?
What numb shivering am I to bear
and what visions will you reward me on the other side?
Your riverbed cracks and crawls
across my crunching brow,
soaking hot rain falling from clouds yawning.

---

[1] Latin for "half the skull." The word *migraine* is the French derivation of
Hemicrania, specifically from "*micrania*." Besides chronic pain, symptoms
can include runny nose, tearing and redness of the eyes, sweating,
drooping eyelids, nausea, vomiting and sensitivity to light.

< 96 >

My useless eyes, blinded, hunt for worries —
I see only night and stumble humbled to a place
where insects and saints command the sky.

S. Gili Post

< 97 >

When I Was Electrocuted

If you have to stop on a rainy night
on your way from New Jersey to Arkansas
for the quickest divorce in the country in 1965
at the only trailer park for miles
    in the Appalachian Mountains
with your four children
who will be stepping in and out of the trailer
in puddles to use the bathroom there
if you are too tired to ground the trailer
when you hook up the electricity —
if your seven-year-old, standing
in the pouring rain, grabs the door handle
of the trailer to come inside . . .

then all of the current
will pass through her right hand,
her right arm, her body,
her right leg and her right foot

and she will be a ground for you

and you will not have
to take her to a doctor you don't know
in a place you have never been
because you know that the current which
she feels in her body for more than
an hour afterwards
will eventually
go away.

Galen Warden

< 98 >

The Exit

For Larry Rue (August 18, 1945-April 7, 2006)

Outside the hospice window, bougainvillea clings
    to stucco walls.
Beyond — eucalyptus, manzanita, avocado groves.

After the cross-country flight, I stroke my brother's hand.
Hi, Larry, I whisper, what are you doing?
Lying here waiting to die.
What are you doing?

★ ★ ★

Our sister suspends a crystal above his third chakra,
We're all waiting to die, she says.
Mother hangs a scapular around his neck,
reads a tractate on the Angel of Death.
I don't give a good goddamn, my brother says.
The nurse changes his morphine drip.

I wave my pocket watch to take away the pain,
force feed him love with some puréed peas.
Wheel him into this last spring's sun,

begin to interview:
Favorite movie? *Citizen Kane.*
Song? *Hey Jude.*
What no longer exists from your childhood?
I expect transistor radio or eight-track tape.
But he's nodding off. I ask again.
Happiness, he says.

★ ★ ★

< 99 >

If the priests hadn't beaten the Latin out of him,
my brother would know that *cure* means *care*.
He came in a Catholic, by God
he'll go out a Catholic, Mother says.
Father Cassidy anoints my brother's head —
Via Vaticum, go slick
and sure into that afterlife
we were so busy preparing for.

Denise Rue

< 100 >

AGAINST HISTORY

The Cross-Dressers of Antietam

Women occasionally disguised themselves as men in order to serve in the American Civil War. Reasons ranged from a sense of duty and honor to country, to simply raising money to send home to family. The Battle of Antietam was the bloodiest day of the Civil War—and twenty-first-century research indicates eight women dressed as men were part of it, two of whom were Mary Galloway and Sarah Emma Edmonds/Franklin Thompson.

Everything becomes private. A bevy of boys is
naked in front of you, in the creek, in a rare moment
between battles. You wish you could join them —
day's a scorcher in these G.D.'d woolens — but you
can't be seen naked. They'll know. Every moment
becomes a challenge, a near-miss, a sigh of relief.

Wipe the sweat from your forehead. This dirty,
bloody mess is well nigh on four years now, and
you have a concern. The young'uns joined in 1861
are now starting to shave, and if this goes on two,
three more years, they're gonna wonder about you.
Some may already wonder about you. Do they whisper
over the campfire at night? Is there an ominous hush
behind the wail of the lone harmonica?

Tying your breasts down is a daily pain, your
private nightmare, but you're still alive, it seems so
little to give, it's really not a bother when you consider
all the young boys who have died, all the flies you've
seen feeding on their corpses, and the fields of body
parts, the blood, the dirt, the roses, the mud, the field,
the violets, the violence, the weary resolve, your fade and
dissolve into grit and resolve. You look at their faces and
wonder — *Am I the only one? Is that a boy? Or am I
looking into a looking glass into my own future?*

< 103 >

Remind yourself you have a name. It may not be your
given name, whatever they're calling you these days,
a world away from dresses and dolls. Someone may say
you don't look a day older than when you came in
but your eyes remain the panes into your pain.

You may never know Antietam numbers: 3,654 killed;
1,771 captured or missing; 18,292 wounded; all in one day:
September 17, 1862, American bloodbath on a steamy
        afternoon.
Now it's 1865: the thrown, the mangled, the war-worn,
    and you.

Women's work is never done. Don't meet their eyes.
Reload your gun.

                                        David Messineo

< 104 >

Mr. Lee Eats an Apple, April 1865

After such devastation
Why should one more death
Matter so much?

Was it the goodness of the man
Or what he stood for?

Or the overwhelming feeling
That so great a war
Deserved an outcome,
Lest all those other deaths
Be rendered meaningless.

He took an apple from the bowl,
But set aside his battle knife.
He would eat it whole.

Raphael Badagliacca

< 105 >

It Is a Sin

Reminiscences from Jean Louise Finch[1]

Long lazy summer days unfurled before me,
    calm nights fluttering on slight breezes,
    a time of broken innocence.

In brightness, fear brazenly surfaced —
    dog gone mad, snarling, as it ambled up the street,
    revealing a gentle protector in a single shot.

Summer to autumn and back again—
    childhood filled with mild surprises
    and a consistency of small changes.

But life would be altered by a lie;
    evil and hatred would sweep in like a heavy flood,
    dammed only by one man's compassion.

Tempers would unfold in the quiet dark,
    shamed faces seeking vengeance under yellow light,
    dispersed by a girl's tender voice.

Villainy hovering on raptor's wings
    would see the Robin fall,
    carrying death, disillusionment, and despair.

One moment in time can define a town's character,
    yet a hero would rise from the ashes in silent flight,
    illuminating the color of truth.

---

[1] The character called Scout in *To Kill a Mockingbird* by Harper Lee.

< 106 >

And I was to find a friend nestled in a hollow
    who put his life at risk for ours,
      bringing justice to a family and redemption to a town.

It was also when I discovered my father,
    empathized with a simple soul
      and fathomed the subtle beauty of mockingbirds.

Denise La Neve

< 107 >

Cinema 24

In dunnest airs of rotting glows,
Pox-cloaked skins and humid holes,
boredom festers curious needs,
tastes of heat or gut-curdling screams,
so upon your entering, please close the door . . .
to my Cinema — Thrill Kill 1924.[1]

Here these halls played festive throughout a stage
of stale lint and rutted days
when all was had and nothing to chance—
the silver spoon, a lucky star,
prodigy and restless-eyed,
we prowled through the minds of men.

As we humans plot the demon seeds,
treacherous thought brings lecherous means.
Froth of boiling bloody bubbles,
the hosts of clotting cranium huddle.
Skies agape and angels bleed,
adrenaline-drunk and fire-eyed,
licking the sweat of fear we breath,
dreaming of gods and grandeur alike,

reveling in the dead stare
while taking you on a dare.

Peter Jaworowski

---

[1] Nathan Leopold, Jr. and Richard Loeb — who became known as
"Leopold and Loeb" — were two wealthy college students who attempted
to commit the perfect crime, murdering fourteen-year-old Bobby Franks in
1924. They were defended by Clarence Darrow in one of the first U.S. cases
to be dubbed "Trial of the Century," and were ultimately sentenced to life
imprisonment. Before the murder, Leopold wrote to Loeb: "A superman
... is, on account of certain superior qualities inherent in him, exempted
from the ordinary laws which govern men. He is not liable for anything he
may do." The case spawned any number of treatments in literature, theater
and cinema.

< 108 >

Freud at Eighty, Convalescing
In the Auersberger Sanatorium

Anatomy is destiny.
—Sigmund Freud

Analogies decide nothing,
it is true, but they can make
one feel more at home.
—Sigmund Freud

More insinuation than accusation,
the cloud of smoke that lingered overhead in
the stale air of the solarium —
But what of the stink that has clung to
his beard for more than forty years?
No nurse has come to halt the primary process
of his first postoperative perfecto.
Its phallic tip snipped ceremoniously,
as though a bris — that the image came
to mind bothered him.
One thing to deliver genial speeches at
B'nai B'rith (the lodge never suspected
an enemy within), quite another were Martha
to light shabbat candles — *verboten!*

Yahweh is but a substitute for father;

as any object, orally fixated on, is replacement
for the breast; as

a good Havana — well ...

He would be the Moses to lead his
people out of the wilderness of
guilt and motivation, except his gods were
several and had Greek names: Oedipus,
Eros, Thanatos, the last at whom
he shook his fist now more than ever.

< 109 >

No nurses had properly attended him after
the first jaw surgery, either; they had gone
home for lunch, and he was left bleeding
all over his clothes until Anna came.

Oh, Anna!

How he needed his daughter
even more than his wife, for those sixteen
years since, an unbroken cathexis between them.
She, more than Martha, knew of the irrepressible
craving the 'tissue rebellion' in his mouth
sought to defend against, mounting its malignant
reaction formation, then of the dolor
of 'the monster'— ill-fitting prostheses that
had eventually replaced his entire right mandible.

Sometimes a cigar teetering on the lip
of an ashtray would roll onto his desk and
burn a hole into the blotter before he noticed.
Sometimes a cigar was clenched between
his teeth as he sat in silence behind
the couch, psychic pain freely associating,
his own compulsion bullying his
superego twenty times each day.

Sometimes a cigar is just a cigar,
he would say.

Brant Lyon

< 110 >

Against Their Will

For people leaving the war
in layers of clothes not yet torn,
outgrown, burnt, stolen or lost,
it was the hottest August ever.
Staying together in groups,
they trudged country roads
like chain gangs, sweat burning
on sun-blistered skin.

On and on they walked,
day after day; falling
into sleep at night, they dreamed
they were still walking. One step
for the sins of the fathers,
one step for the sons, one step
for all those who suffocated
on their own screams.

The children did not yet know
what they had lost
and the old men had forgotten
why they were dying
by the sides of the road.
But the women, refusing
to stay and wait for the houses
they were promised,
walked away from all the lies
planted in the earth.

Refugees forever searching,
they knew they would never again
harvest the fruit in the trees.

< 111 >

These were the wives
alone against their will, mothers
who opened the curtains
to cover their children with stars.
These were the women
who never spoke of their strength—
who took nothing away,
but gave up everything.

Marianne Poloskey

< 112 >

Al Capone's Wife

The men still come, but I realize
they have given up on him. They sit
in the kitchen in their dark suits
and play cards, and I bring them
sandwiches, going in and out of the room
as fast as possible and then listening
to them talk about me through the walls,
all the things they would like to do to me,
because I am being wasted as a woman,
because he no longer knows who I am.
After they go, I wash their plates,
the glasses that never lose the smell of
whiskey. I scrub them as hard as I can
and explain to them about our love,
how it moves backwards now, backwards
from when we met and he made love to me
like I was not in the room, like he was
trying to take something from me while
I had my back turned. After coming back
from prison, his mind half-gone,
he only let me kiss his cheek, and then
just his forehead, and then not at all.
We are left with just touch, my knuckles
brushing against the sleeve of his robe,
and if he looks at me, it's with
thankful eyes, thankful for the gentleness
of a stranger. And sometimes he asks me
for forgiveness, seeing someone else,
seeing the dead in my place. And he
apologizes to the walls, seeing the ghosts
of men he buried. And he apologizes
to the swimming pool, seeing the men
he drowned and choked the life out of.
I tell the silverware what I would tell
the men who still come. This is somehow
what I expected. This is what we want

< 113 >

when we are girls, love that we must
care for. I sleep in a different room
against the wall where I can listen to him
breathing and hear him walking on
the terrace, muttering to the chairs
and table, and I forgive him, and I forgive
the men in dark suits, and I forgive
the dead ones, the ones who colored his skin
with their blood, and I forgive the disease
for destroying him. And I am no longer
screaming. And I am not even whispering.
Just in my mind, I say over and over again:
I forgive you. I forgive you. I forgive you.

Josh Humphrey

< 114 >

The Canticle of the Port Authority Bus Terminal

"The Port Authority Bus Terminal in New York City is the ultimate urban transit station. . . . Encompassing 1.5 million square feet, this facility occupies the blocks bounded by widely spaced Eighth and Ninth Avenues and 40th and 42nd Streets. Knocking out 41st Street entirely, the Port Authority Bus Terminal spans the equivalent of roughly four square blocks at the ground level."
—Redesigning Hell: Preventing Crime and Disorder at the Port Authority Bus Terminal, *by Marcus Felson et al. (Rutgers University, School of Criminal Justice)*

1969–1971

Joe Buck (*Midnight Cowboy*, dir. John Schlesinger, 1969) strutted into town, suede Lonestar swagger for desolate Park Avenue socialites. Ratso Rizzo said only faggots went for that western gear. He knew his city.

★ ★ ★

I came, too, Central N.J. Catholic 14-year-old, a *tabula rasa* in navy blue for the 16th Street Jesuits of St. Francis Xavier High School. First observation when the Port Authority coughed me out onto Eighth Avenue: "Donors Paid" in the blood bank window on the second floor of a building across the street.

★ ★ ★

On the subway: A Hispanic boy about our age asked my friend and me if we had a dime. A.J. checked his watch and said, "3:15." I later reported to my parents we had been mugged.

★ ★ ★

Every morning after the bus dropped off the businessmen and me, I headed right away to the downtown train. One day, with my stomach churning and unable to wait till I reached the school lavatory, I detoured into the bowling alley on the Port Authority's upper floor and then the men's room. There were no doors on the stalls. Years later, I realized why.

< 115 >

★ ★ ★

RATZO: I don't think I can walk anymore. I been falling down a lot. I'm scared.

JOE BUCK: What are you scared of?

RATZO: You know what they do to you when they know you can't . . . when they find out you can't walk.

★ ★ ★

My favorite music at the time was the score of *Hair*, especially Oliver's hit single of "Good Morning, Starshine." *Gliddy gloop gloopy nibby nabby nooby la la la lo lo.* In the early '90s, Oliver and I were employees in the same multinational pharmaceutical company. I was a public affairs manager. He worked in sales.

★ ★ ★

I always talked to strangers: the ones manning card tables along the perimeter of the main concourse to publicize their causes. The Hare Krishnas dispensed tasty cookie balls. The John Birch Society dispensed nothing tasty. The National Organization for the Reform of Marijuana Laws dispensed nothing (in the public space).

> A panhandler sings
> Hare Krishna
> At the evening rush hour.

> They travel at competitive speeds:
> Commuters and cockroaches.

> Outside the drugstore,
> Jesus spreads the gospel
> Of cannabis.

< 116 >

Simon says, "Here I am,
The only living boy in New York."

★ ★ ★

Movie theater marquee on 42nd Street:

I, a Woman
The Devil in Miss Jones

1978–1982

To cap a summer night on the town, David (R.I.P.), K. and I sought out an Eighth Avenue trash bar. It wasn't hard to find. After nearly a decade of commuting to Manhattan, I had never been inside one before, having believed my mother I was a sophisticated New Yorker displaced in the suburbs.

★ ★ ★

A dusty black man nodded off in a wheelchair outside the peepshow. A week later, same spot, still napping.

★ ★ ★

The street vendor
Lays fresh meat on his grill.
A cat mourns.

★ ★ ★

The corner God-hawker wielded his King James like a cudgel. Did he wear the dowdy suit jacket (brown? faded charcoal?) to appear more respectable or just to hide his tracks?

★ ★ ★

The New Jersey Turnpike shoveled travelers into the Port Authority's polluted throat. So did the Minnesota Strip.

< 117 >

A 12-year-old girl
In lavender vinyl
Cries black streaks of tears.

★ ★ ★

Movie theater marquee on 42nd Street:

Revenge of Drunken Master
Mad Monkey Kung Fu

2005–2006
Fans lined up on 42nd Street for Donny Osmond's show at B.B. King Blues Club & Grill. Four doors away at the American Airlines Theater, Harry Connick Jr. starred in a revival of *The Pajama Game*.

★ ★ ★

I wandered into the Port Authority bowling alley for the first time in 35 years. A slender waiter in East Village black balanced a plate of sesame chicken. A table was dressed with fresh linen and silver chafing dishes for Happy Hour. A countertop placard advertised children's birthday parties. I strolled into the men's room. Every stall had a door.

★ ★ ★

Movie theater marquee on 42nd Street:

Brokeback Mountain
Capote

Postscript

Joe Buck was found dead in Miami.

Joel Allegretti

< 118 >

A Hack's Elusive Love

or, Arthur Miller Lives

Surprisingly, in my universe of taxi driving
intersecting with New York's — spaced-out humanity —
I'm still intrigued by otherworldly characters

I encounter behind my head. Met a fish food salesman
from Secaucus, hauled him in early evening twilight
during rush hour's syncopated prelude —

when whimsy surrenders to horn-honking & road rage.
My passenger requested a ride to The Big Dinghy,
an upscale bar located somewhere near Water Street.

Navigating my yellow cab on a schizophrenic avenue
between farting buses & Subarus, I peered at Mister Jersey
from my rearview mirror. Aquamarine eyes &
      a crooked smile

embellished an adorable cartoon face
projecting a distinct sense of self. Out of pure boredom
or my usual free-floating anxiety, I decided to probe

his Garden State brain, this fish food salesman
salivating for high-priced cocktails. Inquiring
about the pros & cons of a fishy profession —

selling morsels to sustain creatures of the aquarium —
the man simply stated, "It can be a lonely job"—
inspiring him to jabber about lucrative sales territory

up & down Atlantic's eastern shore. "I hawk
pet stores in Delaware one day, Philly the next!"
Listening with my right ear — while challenging a truck

< 119 >

over a merging lane change, I mused to myself —
a loneliness, all for the sake of little mineral crystals
thrown into glass prisons of tropical blues & gold —

simple sustenance for fresh water swimmers
trapped among wavering weeds & pebbles.
"Do you have a wife?" I selfishly spouted out —

anxious perhaps to hook a future companion.
"She puts up with the traveling aspect of my life."
Disappointed, I pondered my own traveling aspect.

A competitive race, always seeking customers
for my backseat, even loud-mouthed shrimps
shouting addresses with patronizing contempt!

At our destination, depositing Willie Loman-of-the-Sea
before a bustling watering hole
frequented by bankers & loose women —

he paid me through the partition window
tossing over a handsome tip
& personal business card

decorated with smiling mermaids. My worn eyes
made instant love as the lost catch faded into the night.
I dove back into my ocean of redundancy, fishing for fares.

Davidson Garrett

< 120 >

Prelude 9/10/11

9,10,11,
12,
2001

nine ten
2001:
my mother
died
10:30
pm
The sleepless night
my space odyssey (after Kubrick)
had begun
before
9/11 @
just at...
930 am or so,
or so.....

The midst of mourning:
tranquil;

quiet;

undone.

This morning like no
other:

my brother's birthday

is **9/11/01.**

< 121 >

Disturbed
and
shaken

by the arrival of the funeral director
only to be told something about
the world trade center:

TURN ON THE TV
he implored !!!!!
I watched as you
heard the bang of the bodies
hit the floor,
as the reporters
transmitted their stories
as the bodies rained down
before the buildings
fell....

My mother's body
was moved about midnight or 1am,
as the hospice staff took notes.
Then
the mass was postponed
the cemetery closed
in Queens (as another Calvary)
inaccessible
from New Jersey
until the following day
so,
everything
was postponed

< 122 >

9,10,11,

12 in a matter

of minutes
numbers
move
as they

coalesce
into
i
n

f
i
n
i
t
y......

Daniel P. Quinn

< 123 >

BETWEEN US

In The Bath

The water runs warm, steams up my mirror, windows.
   I run it long,
splash it to heat the bottom of the tub so as not
to shock my delicate little feet with the cruelty of cold,
   ridged porcelain.
Lotions bustle forward on my racks, many, many bottles
   vie to be chosen.
They crowd the four-shelved, spring-loaded,
   floor-to-ceiling rack
that beckons from the corner, they lurk beneath the last shelf
and peek out from around the corners of the draping curtain.
Bars and poufs dangle from the showerhead rack,
dance in the happy, warm spray.

They do not make a thing that I will not pour
over my head, believing the miracle of the model's hair,
the softness of her skin and the slippery oil sensation
that draws me most of all.

The scents of the bottles waft around me in the steam,
carry me somewhere else where I ought to have been,
where I do not suffer the indignity of having to scrub
   my own back,
where brushes and blades are wielded on my behalf.
I raise my arms, turn, bend, luxuriate
in the scented steam, the elaborate fixtures
of the ritual bath, its large pools and soaring plants,
its echoing yards of tile inhabited only by myself
   and my attendants.
My scalp is massaged very, very slowly, then conditioned
   with pineapples and sage,
the hair brushed gently, gently, so that its soaking
   wetness parts
easily for the comb, no stretched broken split ends here.

< 127 >

Shining sharpness flashes toward raised arms, leaves silk
in its wake along the calves previously massaged
with a potion of volcanic ash scented lightly with lemon
and suspended in a matrix of softeners. A heart-shaped stone
diligently rubs away unpleasantness at the edges of my feet,
and a small sea sponge, saturated with acids extracted
from the finest over-ripe fruit, caresses my face,
        smoothing away
the older skin of yesterday, bringing today's glow
        to the surface.

Hands — impossible to tell how many — knead
        and stroke me
with a cleanser permeated with the essence of oatmeal
        and honey, and, yes,
I am oiled slick as seal's skin with a heavy emulsion
        made to cling
past the shower, to soak into the skin and leave
        softness everywhere
following the drying dabs of towels. I am rinsed once,
        twice, more,
first with warm water, then cool, then cold to smooth
        ruffled hair,
sluice away the remains of the ritual,
leave the cleansed body pink and ready
for the drier ordeals of makeup and perfume.

< 128 >

The curtain swoops grandly aside and I blink in cold,
    wet dismay
at the tiny ugly bathroom, its faded '50s pink-and-blue
    tile, the
bizarre hot pink blooms that dangle from curled-edge
wallpaper, wondering
if the bath slaves remembered to warm my towels
    before vanishing.

Dorothy Alexander

< 129 >

Origami

If only the history of our
time and space could
fold back into itself
like origami,

you and I could
touch and crease together,
folded back from needs and nows
into a paper bird of our love
that exists apart from reason.

If only your blue paper side
could be pressed over
my yellow paper side,
the fibers that have
separated us could
join and lock
into a real dream of
flying away

that every
paper bird
dreams.

Galen Warden

< 130 >

Pears

When you are here the pears
in their bowl ripen
differently, their flesh flecked brown,
throbbing yellow.   I like
how your footsteps force
dust bunnies further into corners,
your hands stack spoons in their allotted space,
the way a family should fit,
not just helter skelter, so now
when I reach in to spoon sugar into my tea,
no serrated edges or rusted blades.
When you come back I'll poach pears in wine and sugar.
You'll praise their grainy silk and I won't shatter
the cut glass bowls when I rinse them in scalding suds.
I won't.

Denise Rue

< 131 >

She Walks Softly There in Silence

She walks softly there in silence,
Bathed in dark and light and blue,
But mainly in her sadness.

By the window
She slips lightly, like the tide
That crosses nightly
'Tween the watch-house and the bay.

And she makes breathing soft and silent,
From a weathered chair,
Its comfort broken by long years in salt air . . .
Seasoned nights by scent of sea-straw,
And the distance, longing there.

George C. Harvilla

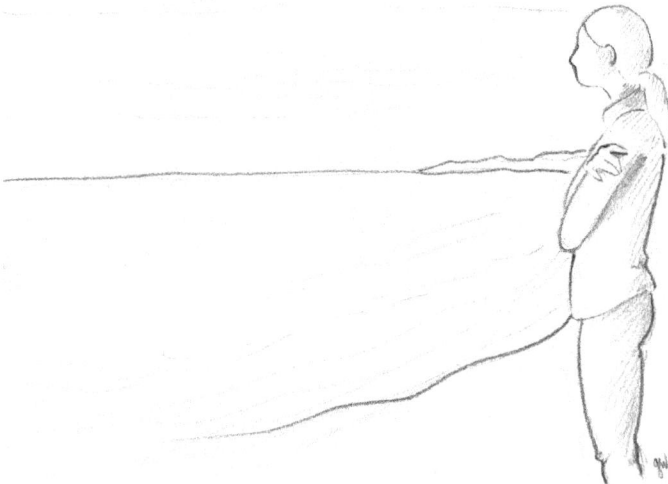

< 132 >

Love

Don

Love is in the eyes
and on the skin.
Love does not blink.
Love rushes in.

Blushes and blinks,
barbarous bliss,
love begins and ends
with a kiss.

Love

Colleen

love appeals to the eyes
love congeals on the thighs
love retreats with a whine
love remains in the mind

Donald Zirilli and C. D. Russell

< 133 >

Utility

Cursor, blinking in his
Iris, a swarm of blur and
Splendor, humming in the
Twilight; he gives birth.

Trembling fingertips
Sculpt his creation
Like a Navajo at
Her wheel;

Megabytes pressing on
His mind, his choices
Infinite, her colors
Bleeding into one
Another on
Her tapestry —

She asks him
To rest upon her
Blanket, but he,
Of a different
Fantasy,

Hangs himself with
A cable.

Catherine Cimillo Cavallone

< 134 >

Sound Theory

In theory, an *I love you*
called from the second-story window
could travel

into infinity. Depending,
of course, on its amplitude.
I loved you more,
so my *I love you*s reached further.

Maybe,
on a good day,
your *I love you*s moseyed up
to bump a rainbow's arc.
Maybe, one
brushed the redwood's stiff fringe.
One
thumbed the wing of a red-tailed hawk.

My *I love you*s found the absence of God,
bolted straight through space
past nebulas and quasars.
My *I love you*s were sucked into black holes
where neither matter nor light escapes.

Denise Rue

< 135 >

Magyar Man

I fell fast and hard for Magyar man —

Dark his eyes, dark his hold,
Black his tumbling mane like coal.
Deep his smell, like heresy;
Lips stronger than Coffee Sulawesi.

I fell into some strange longing,
Sweet the nectar of its calling;
Poisoned by seductive power
Were our stolen days, nights and hours.

I fell under some strange spell,
Denying staunchly each time I fell,
So I believed I held the reins,
Yet my beliefs were all in vain.

I fell fast and hard for Magyar man —
And I will flee him if I can.
His mark is singed upon my soul,
Black his tumbling mane like coal . . .

Aza Derman

< 136 >

Rain Falling

You are the rain falling
stealing glimpses through my window
fingers longingly trailing the panes
in this youngest hour of the night

Your whisper
gentle
and constant
lulls my secluded heart
as your filmy embrace secures
that place wherein I seek my sanctuary

You are the waters
sent by those sworn guardians
of faith
in love
that I might be sanctified

Your touch
tender
and sacred
has been my redemption
and the morrow's pure light
illuminates pools of remembrances
offered
by one honorable
and true

K. Elizabeth Costa

< 137 >

Untitled 1

breath marks on the window
poems on the coffee table.

Untitled 2

She was an old woman
before this world began
and I am awake
meeting her in the valley.

Untitled 4

Crushed bug almost made its way
across the pillow, almost
onboard.

The affair long over.

Gene Myers

< 138 >

Parasitoid

She slips away as silently as she came.
Soon the eggs laid within hatch . . .

Hungry, ever so hungry,
young legs scrabbling to find purchase,
gnashing mandibles!

The greedy, bloated children

feasting, grow**ing**,

sucking on juices — delicious torment.
Prolonged sweet suffering,
ever so s-l-o-w-l-y draining the life away.

Seething . . . *squirming* . . . **Gnawing**

Clinging and spasming
in an ecstasy of overindulgence.

Survival as Death Incarnate—
Eat, my children!

Then a throbbing metamorphosis . . .
in perfect synchronization to
the host's final convulsive moments.

Emergence by moonlight —
Adults now, they couple madly
in shadowy swarms.

Within hours the search begins . . .
In an atmosphere of charged anticipation,
a strange attraction—
tormentor to unwilling victim.

< 139 >

A female alights ever so softly,
  then thrusts in a climax of savage lust,
    piercing her intended,
      spewing forth a viscous ichor,
        her evil spawn.

The host shudders in a convulsive
  prologue of things to come.

She slips away as silently as she came.
  Soon the eggs laid within hatch . .

Paul Nash

< 140 >

The Harvestman

Day fell. The cooling sun careened and set,
an orange flare behind the broiling hill.
August is full upon the town, and yet
the lakeside grove is desolate and still.

No gravestones bear my surname here—
(my forebears have vanished to scattered dust)—
yet this is where I contemplate a bier,
a monument, a poet's shattered bust.

This burial ground of proud and prudent Scot
is now a blasted place of toppled stones,
storm-blasted trunks and layered, fungal rot,
tree ears and bell-shaped mushrooms white as bones.

The ancient limestone markers, tumble-tossed,
cast off like cards at the end of a game,
speak of loves played and grand illusions lost,
fragmented now to letters from a name,

scrabbled by giants or angry, spiteful youth,
treefall, or lightning's vengeful, jabbing pen,
first from surname pulled like a broken tooth,
birth date from death, the where of it, the when

now jumbled like a madman's ransom note.
Words carved in stone as certain history
confound the reader now in jumbled quote,
turning church'd facts to puzzled mystery.

Upon an obelisk of limestone, cold
with the chill of glacial remembering,
beneath the wizened shade of maples, old
with a century's Novembering,

< 141 >

a host of Harvestmen ride skitter-skit,
legs tracing Braille of infant's monument.
Daddy-Long-Legs! sly arachnids, unfit
for sunlight, silent raptors, demon-sent—

Why do you writhe and twine those wiry limbs
(too many to count as they crouch and leap)?
Why herd like worshippers entranced by hymns,
then fly like clerks with appointments to keep?

One moment you're here in a skittering tide;
then, as my shadow touches your eyes,
you race to the obelisk's other side,
the way a tree'd squirrel is caught by surprise.

We play out this Harvestman hide-and-seek,
round and round the moss-fringed, ancient grave,
'til I can almost hear these monsters, meek
and voiceless, moving in a song, a wave

of primal hungering. Bad luck, cursed crops,
they say, if you kill one. Better to dread
their venomless fangs, their sinister drops
from overhanging branch or dusty bed!

What do they eat? What do those tiny eyes
seek out and chase amid marble and slate?
Leaf-litter bugs, dead things of any size,
trapped beneath fangs and feeders (eight!).

Are you the harvesters of suicides?
Do the soul buds of babies appease you?
Do you drink the tears of abandoned brides?
Does the mist from rotting coffins please you?

< 142 >

Your mouths are not for speaking, Harvestmen.
Your secrets, like the truth behind the stones
(how did they really die, and why, and when?)
are told in your thousand-leg dance on bones.

Night now. The knowing moon will rise and set,
an umber globe behind the misty hill.
Pregnant autumn is in the air, and yet
the still-green grove is desolate and still.

All night, ten thousand eyes are watching here,
shepherds tending their ectoplasmic fold,
forty thousand spider tendrils, fear
incarnate, soul vampires, patient and old!

Harvestman, Harvestman, whom do you seek?

Brett Rutherford

< 143 >

This Much I Know

Not many of them, it's true,
but certain poems
rattle your body's timber,
smack you about an instant

like a cartoon fish that suspends
itself in midair, slapping its tail
across your cheeks, having
been stolen from its ocean,

before, with a splash, returning
to a reef or a drifting tangle of weed.
Stunned, you step into a lifetime,
lips flecked with fish scales,

skin slick with new slime.
Everything you feel is different now:
The air that wraps about your fingers
as you plow them through an hour,

the way moonlight knots your hair,
even a mosquito that locks its needle
in your skin — the itch tingles deeper.

S. Thomas Summers

< 144 >

Dreams

I thought the love we shared
would drive our dreams together,
help us rise beyond the rift between.
Here is my dream, I said, and promised,
and delivered, a Ship of Dreams
upon which you and I first picked up steam.

I will place you on the stage
in the stillness of a spotlight
while remembering who you were—
dreams fade — who you'd become
dreams rage — how we'd been
dreams age — how we'd change

Here we cross again across the dreamscape
drawn like Gothic vampires to a neck nape
Providence and Fate entwine us slow
Let my words like feathers wisp below . . .
linger . . .
go.

Can't spell *community* without *m-u-t-i-n-y*
those who've captained long enough well know.
Here is my dream, you said, promised, delivered.
Yes, I support the spreading of your voice —
just remember, separate travel was your choice.

Still I will see you on the stage
in the stillness of a microphone
remembering us sailing as one
dreams fade — tsunami, rift
dreams rage — tidal shift
dreams age — the weight, the sift

< 145 >

Do clouds feel when they touch in dreamscape?
Is their touch a kiss across the neck nape?
Providence and Fate still lock us down
As espresso machines again drown
my words,
your words,
our words.

David Messineo

< 146 >

The Watcher

The love that does not touch, that makes
    no penetration,
requires no mirror back to verify
that what is real is real.

This love excels all lovers.
The unmailed letter superior
    to the letter returned unread,
the passion that leaves the eye
    as a gift to beauty.

Love thus, in secret, and love again.
Enlarge the heart
    (O it has many chambers!)
If the loved one be as oblivious
    as a fieldstone,
so be it! Moss clings, sun warms,
water wears down—there are many ways
to make love to granite.
You say the love you give
is not returned to you?
Leave to the bankers
the keeping of balances,
the squeezing out
    of interest.

Love is returned, somehow,
in the ease of future loving,
the cavalcade of youth
pressing on by
as you watch from the café window,

marveling there is so much in you
beaming back at them,
so many qualities and curves,
neck napes and striding legs,

< 147 >

sungold, raven black & pumpkin hair,
and the gemstone eyes
of onyx, turquoise, emerald and hazel —

what would they be
if you were not there to love them?
what coalmine darkness
    would they walk in,
if we did not spark them
with our admiration.

Be not jealous of touching.
Does not the air,
    thick with the ghosts
        of the world's love cries
press down upon you?
Do not the star lamps
warm you? Does not the tide
crash out your name
upon the lonely cliffs?

Without desire, the universe
would cool to neutrons;
the whirligig of being
would slow to a stop.
So storm out! radiate
your unsought affections,
the passing poet, taking nothing,
    giving all.

Brett Rutherford

< 148 >

ABOUT THE POETS & ARTISTS

DOROTHY ALEXANDER has a BA in psychology from Montclair State University and is completing her Masters in Social Work at New York University, where she is due to graduate in May of this year. She was a journalist for *The News of Paterson*. Dorothy has been an active member of the "Palisades Poetry Scene" since the 1990s, when she hosted a poetry reading series in Teaneck, New Jersey. Her poetry has appeared in *Sensations Magazine*.

JOEL ALLEGRETTI is the author of *The Plague Psalms* (2000), now in its third edition, and *Father Silicon*, selected by the *Kansas City Star* as one of the 100 Noteworthy Books of 2006. Both books are published by The Poets Press. His newly-released third collection, *Thrum*, is a chapbook of poems, prose poems and brief poetic essays about musical instruments, published by Poets Wear Prada (2010). Allegretti's work has appeared in *New York Quarterly, Margie, Rattapallax, Laurel Review, Art/Life Limited Editions, Descant, Confrontation, Xcp Cross-Cultural Poetics, River Oak Review*, and many other national journals. He is represented in the noted anthology *Chance of a Ghost* (Helicon Nine Editions, 2005). His poem in that collection received an Honorable Mention in the 2006 edition of *The Year's Best Fantasy and Horror*, published by St. Martin's Press. A Pushcart Prize nominee, he was one of three writers selected for the 2005 inaugural Visible Word, a collaboration of literary and visual artists sponsored by the DeBaun Center for the Performing Arts, Stevens Institute of Technology. In April 2009, Kean University in New Jersey presented the world premiere of a song cycle based on Allegretti's poetry: *A Cycle by the Sea*, composed by Frank Ezra Levy, distinguished cellist with the Radio City Music Hall Orchestra, whose symphonic work is available in the American Classics series on the Naxos label. Please visit his website at www.joelallegretti.com.

RAPHAEL BADAGLIACCA is the author of two books: *Father's Day: Encounters with Everyday Life* (www.fathersdaybook.com) and *The Yogi Poems and Other Celebrations of Local Baseball* (www.yogipoems.com). The New Jersey Arts Collective elected to transform *Father's Day* into

< 149 >

a staged event involving three actors. He also staged portions of the book as a one-man show off-off Broadway at the SoHo Playhouse. Two of his pieces from *Father's Day* were recently broadcast on National Public Radio's *The Green Space* (2009), and the first, entitled "Bedtime Story," was rebroadcast on WNYC's *Evening Music*, hosted by Terrance McKnight. He has performed his poetry and prose in several venues in the tristate area. His most recent poems have appeared in *The Louisville Review* and *The Sanskrit Literary Magazine*. Raphael writes two blogs: www.moviesightings.com and www.booksightings.com. He is the founder/owner of a software company.

CATERINA BELVEDERE has been active in the "Palisades," or "Hudson River," poetry scene since 1996. She wears many hats, as writer and performer, mother, healer, teacher, and artist. Born to Italian parents, Caterina's love of life through the spoken word, music, dance, art, opera, architecture, and cooking are, in her words, "a natural inheritance." As an adult, her tai chi and Taoist studies have sparked a keen interest in Chinese poetry, particularly the works of Lao Tzu and Chuang Zu. Diverse poetic influences also include Walt Whitman, Giuseppe Ungheretti, Emily Dickinson, and Gabriele D'Anunzio, among others. Caterina's poetry has appeared in *The Rift Arts Forum Publication* and *Sensations Magazine*. She is a practicing shiatsu therapist and energy healer. Current projects include a cookbook of old Calabrian recipes and a collection of healing remedies handed down in her family. Ms. Belvedere lives in Bergen County, New Jersey, with her two daughters and a Maltese pup named Snowball, aka "Beni."

JOHN CHORAZY was the editor of *The Ever Dancing Muse* from 1993 to 2003. He has facilitated writing workshops as a teaching artist for the Artists in Education program sponsored by the New Jersey State Council on the Arts, as well as the New Jersey Music Society's Literacy Through Jazz program. His poems have appeared widely in literary journals and the Small Press. *Poems for Lunch*, an assortment of short works, was published in 1997 by Who Who Who Publishing. His collection *Walking Through My Father's Garden* won the William Paterson University English Department Chapbook Competition and was published in 2006 by WPU. He has read his work at various venues in the tristate area and has coordinated events in New Jersey including

< 150 >

a monthly literary series at The Montclair Public Library, as well as one at The Mug and the Bean in Rutherford. A resident of Montclair, he presently teaches English Literature at Pequannock Township High School in New Jersey.

CATHERINE CIMILLO CAVALLONE is a full-time English teacher and mom who enjoys creative writing during rare moments of free time, reading fiction and researching Victorian architecture throughout New Jersey. Her poetry has appeared in *Four Walls, Sensations Magazine,* and *The Rift Arts Forum Publication.* She has been featured at the North Jersey Literary Series and other tristate venues, and she participated in John Salacan's *The Muse Pool,* a multimedia theatrical production of music and poetry staged in 2002, starring eleven poets whose work appears in this anthology. Cathy has also been a Civil War reenactor for the last six years with her husband, George, and son, Michael.

K. ELIZABETH COSTA (formerly K. Elizabeth Sieradzki) has independently published two chapbooks, *Angels with One Wing* and *Paths of Desire.* Her work has appeared in several literary publications, including *Sensations Magazine, The Ever Dancing Muse,* and *The Plowman.* Her poem "No One Is Innocent" was featured on WFDU-FM's radio broadcast of *The Poet's Corner.* She has performed her original work in venues ranging from book stores and cafés to small theaters. She is grateful to her husband, Michael, and daughter, Olivia Grace, for their support and inspiration, and owes them her eternal love and devotion.

AZA DERMAN is a New York eclectic, avid reader, and history buff. She recently opened an eBay store called Azantia Jewelry (www.stores.ebay.com/Azantia-Jewelry), launching her own unique product line. She plans to pursue her twin passions of forensic anthropology and Scandinavian archaeology. Currently, Aza resides in Westchester, New York, and nurtures an incurable addiction to poetry.

TOM FITZPATRICK lives in Pompton Lakes, New Jersey, where he wanders the nearby woodlands in search of subject matter for his art work. A graduate of William Paterson and New York Universities, he taught art in the Teaneck public schools for thirty years. He has

< 151 >

illustrated several archaeological books and numerous other publications, and has exhibited locally.

ESTRELLA GABRIE-GARCIA came to the United States from Honduras in 1954, initially settling in Brooklyn but moving to New Jersey in 1961. She was a member of POET-X, a five-person poetry performance group founded in 1997; the other four members were Joel Allegretti, Eddie Rivera, Joseph Andrew Sapia, and John J. Trause, all of whom appear in this anthology. Estrella is an actress and poet, and has appeared in several films. She also has an interest in photography, and one of her photos was used on the cover of *Sensations Magazine*, Issue 19: "Millennium Turning" (1999). Estrella's poetry has appeared in *Sensations Magazine* and in *The Rift Arts Forum Publication*.

DAVIDSON GARRETT is a native of Shreveport, Louisiana, currently living in New York City. He is the author of a collection of poetry and prose entitled *King Lear of the Taxi* (Advent Purple Press, 2006). In August 2009, he was featured in Joel Allegretti's tribute to Leonard Cohen: *You Know Who I Am*, at the Cornelia Street Café in Greenwich Village. He trained for the theater at the American Academy of Dramatic Arts and is a member of Screen Actor's Guild, Actor's Equity, and AFTRA. Davidson has appeared on television in such shows as *All My Children*, *The Guiding Light*, *As the World Turns*, *Law and Order*, *Oz*, and *Spin City*. As a stage actor, he has toured extensively in the United States and Europe, and has performed in verse dramas by T. S. Eliot, W. H. Auden, and William Shakespeare. In March of 2008, Flashgun Films of Great Britain released a short film entitled *Taxi Driver*, narrated by Davidson and using poems from his collection. It was screened at two international film festivals that year (Google *King Lear of the Taxi* on YouTube). His literary works have appeared in *The New York Times*, *Xavier Review* (New Orleans), *The Episcopal New Yorker*, *Sensations Magazine*, *The Unknown Writer*, and in the *Friends For Life* and *The Wild Angels* anthologies. Online, his poetry can be found at www.poetryvlog.com, www.BigCityLit.com, and on the website of the Beat Museum in San Francisco. To subsidize his art, Davidson has been a New York City taxi driver for over thirty years.

< 152 >

JONATHAN HALL is a poet, fiction writer, and critic originally from Rochester, New York. He completed an MFA in fiction writing and a PhD in American Literature at Cornell University. His work has appeared in *White Pelican Review, Poetry Motel, Another Chicago Magazine, Sou'wester, The Hawaii Review,* and elsewhere, and he has been nominated for a Pushcart Prize. Hall currently teaches English at York College, City University of New York.

PATRICK HAMMER, JR. is co-facilitator for the Wild Angels Poets and Writers Group based at the Cathedral Church of Saint John the Divine in Manhattan. He is also a workshop leader for the Fort Lee-based Main Street Poets and Writers, and is moderator for the Page Turners Book Discussion Group, also in Fort Lee. His work has appeared widely in small press publications both in the United States and Europe. He has published a number of chapbooks.

GEORGE C. HARVILLA is a recipient of the Hemingway Prize for Literature, winner of the U.S. Masters Poetry Prize, and two-time recipient of the *Atlanta Review*'s International Merit Award for Poetry. He was featured at the Dodge Poetry Festival in "Poets Among Us" in 2002. A classically-trained percussionist, George has played with the Dresden Opera and the Bolshoi Ballet. In the non-classical realm, he has performed/toured with Tito Puente, Mongo Santamaria, Billy Preston, Sun Ra, Trilok Gurtu, Harry Chapin, the Original Gipsy Kings, Crowded House, the Divinyls, and Midnight Oil, among others. His body of work includes soundtracks for the films *Gettysburg, A Midnight Clear, Gangs of New York,* and *Last of the Mohicans.* Additionally, he is the primary lyricist for the English version of Janek Ledecky's international hit musical *Hamlet: The Rock Opera* and lyricist for Ondrej Soukup's modern opera *Joan of Arc.*

JOSH HUMPHREY spends his days as a librarian and archivist, a job in which he finds much poetry. He was runner-up in the Allen Ginsberg Poetry Competition for 2009, and has received honorable mention for this award on three previous occasions. He is a past recipient of the Merlyn Girard Poetry Prize, and he won the America at War Poetry Contest sponsored by *Sensations Magazine* in 2004. He was one of the inaugural co-features for the William Carlos Williams

< 153 >

Poetry Cooperative in Rutherford, New Jersey (January 2006). Some of his work will appear in an upcoming issue of *Paterson Literary Review*, and his poems have been published in *The New Plains Review, The Talking River Review, The Journal of New Jersey Poets, Lips, The Rift, Soundings East, Lullwater Review, Sensations Magazine, Mentil Soup*, and *Ibbetson Street*. Josh has lived all his life in and around Kearny, New Jersey — his involvement with local history and legend has greatly inspired his writing. He is currently enjoying his one-year-old daughter, Cate, with his lovely wife, Jen, and poodle, Pancho.

PETER JAWAROWSKI first thinks of himself as an explorer of possibilities. He finds excitement in many physical activities — racing motocross, practicing tai chi, cross-country running, skiing, skating, as well as traveling throughout Europe, North America, China, and India — he has literally been around the world once! Back home, in the latter 1990s, Peter was the production director for *The Rift Arts Forum Publication*. In this capacity, he co-hosted a number of poetry readings and special performance events in New Jersey and New York, and was influential in the Palisades/Hudson River poetry movement. Peter helped organize *Rift*-sponsored monthly literary series, among them "A Drop of Wisdom," "The Creative Circle," and the "Dead Poets Revival," at Marc's Cheesecake and Café Local (both in Englewood, New Jersey), and Borders Books (Paramus, New Jersey). Other *Rift* reading series were held in places like Archetypus (Edgewater NJ), Café Eclectic (Montclair NJ), and Spesso Lounge (North Bergen NJ). Peter helped organize special arts events at the Hudson Grill and at CBGB's Gallery (both in NYC). He took part in live and recorded radio recitals, ran open readings at the Dodge Poetry Festival, and initiated several mixed-media art exhibitions encompassing a variety of artists in Jersey City and New York City. Peter was also often seen in Philadelphia performing and reciting poetry at literary and creative art events at The Raven Café, The Black Abbey, The Loop Lounge, The Black Banana, The Middle East, and The Painted Bride Arts Center, among others. His poetry has appeared in *The Rift Arts Forum Publication, Hipnosis*, and *Sensations Magazine*.

< 154 >

THOMAS D. JONES is the author of two books of poetry: *Voices from the Void* (2009) and *Genealogy X* (2000), both published by The Poet's Press. In 2008, his poetry appeared in the online journal *Language and Culture*, and in *Appleseeds*, an anthology about the American experience. His other online poetry credits include *Raintiger* (www.raintiger.com), *The Surface*, *Scrivener's Pen*, and *Write-Away*. Tom's work also has been published in numerous print magazines throughout the United States. Originally from northern New Jersey, Tom has a BA in English from Seton Hall University and an MA in publishing studies from New York University. After twelve years in the publishing field, he changed careers and now teaches ESL and computer skills at adult education programs in Rhode Island. He was the founder, publisher, and poetry editor of the journal *Wings* (print and online) through 2002.

DENISE LA NEVE writes both poetry and fiction. Her work has most recently appeared in the international journal *The Istanbul Literary Review* (www.ilrmagazine.net) January 2010, and in the 2008 and 2009 issues of *The Rutherford Red Wheelbarrow Anthology*, along with unpublished work by William Carlos Williams, among others. Denise won the *Sensations Magazine* Best Newcomer contest for poetry (2005), as well as that publication's short story contest (2007). She has co-authored several poems with her husband, Paul Nash, creating a new and distinct voice. Denise co-hosts the longstanding North Jersey Literary Series in Teaneck, New Jersey, which features poets and musicians. She has herself been featured at numerous poetry venues. Denise danced with Kleber deFreitas in several performances of *Night and Day*, based on original choreography by Fred Astaire and Ginger Rogers, and she appeared in John Salacan's *The Muse Pool* (2002) as both poet and dancer. She participated in two photographic exhibitions of tristate poets entitled *Inside Out* (2006 and 2007).

RICHARD LORANGER is a writer, performer, visual artist, and all-around squeaky wheel, currently residing in Oakland, California. He is the author of *Poems for Teeth* (We Press, 2005), which Bob Holman calls "one of the most extraordinary and virtuosic poetic feats since Francis Ponge took on *Soap*," as well as *The Orange Book* and eight chapbooks, including *Hello Poems* and *The Day Was Warm and Blue*. Recent work can be found in *Correspondence 1 & 2* and *CLWN WR 42*

< 155 >

& 45, and the upcoming *Uphook Press Anthology #2*. He wants only a calm moment.

ROY LUCIANNA is a published poet, musician, and exhibited painter/sculptor. He has been writing seriously for fifteen years, was an active member of the "Palisades Poetry Movement" in the 1990s, and an editor for *The Rift Arts Forum Publication* from 1996-1999. He also contributed poetry and artwork for *The Rift*, and hosted the Rift-sponsored "Dead Poets Revival" series, comparing the lives and work of two historical poets each month. Roy and ten other poets who appear in these pages performed in *The Muse Pool*, a multimedia theatrical production of music and poetry staged by John Salacan in 2002. Roy is self-employed as a teacher and practitioner of Taiji Quan, Qigong, meditation, qi healing, Taoist arts, astrology, and shamanic counseling. He teaches courses and lectures on topics from poetry to mythology to Chinese brush painting, sculpture, and art history. At the core, he is a Taoist: "all streams, all activities, flow as one with the Tao — the source of creativity." Please visit his website at http://roylucianna.info.

BRANT LYON writes poetry, fiction, reviews, and music. His poems have appeared in *Rattle, Lullwater Review, BigCityLit, Medicinal Purposes,* and other literary journals. Select works have been anthologized in *The Company We Keep* (Poet Warrior 2003), *A Cautionary Tale* (Uphook Press 2008), and *The Rutherford Red Wheelbarrow Anthology* (2008 and 2009). Brant has put together a collection entitled *Your Infidel Eyes* (Poets Wear Prada 2006), now in its second printing, based on his love affair with oasis life in Egypt. He hosts and curates the poetry and music series Hydrogen Jukebox in New York City. His "poemusic" has been recorded on several CDs, including *Beauty Keeps Laying Its Sharp Knife Against Me*. Brant is co-editor at Uphook Press. He grew up in New Jersey, but now lives in Brooklyn.

DAVID MESSINEO — poet, performance artist, poetry editor, and publisher — has been active in the New Jersey poetry scene across five decades from 1979, when he was poetry editor of a high school literary magazine, to 2010, with his role as one of five editors for this anthology. During this time, his creation of and volunteer service to *Sensations*

< 156 >

Magazine since 1987 earned him first place in the national American Literary Magazine Awards on two occasions. Then, in 2009 he received the distinguished Jefferson Award for Public Service — one of only 26 individuals from the State of New Jersey to be so honored. Most recently, all 50 *Sensations Magazine* issues and all of his poetry books were nationally archived in the research/reading collections of the Library of Congress. His poetry has been published in numerous literary journals and national magazines on four continents, and in seven books (*First Impressions, Suburban Gothic, A Taste of Italy, A Taste of Brazil, Restoration, Formal,* and the still-in-progress *Historiopticon*). In order to provide poets with opportunities to share their work in public, he has hosted over 700 events in 48 states across 24 years. He wrote and contributed his recent poem "Dreams" specifically for this anthology.

GENE MYERS is a poet and journalist living in northern New Jersey. He writes a syndicated weekly column, and his essays and interviews appear in more than 40 newspapers. Gene is the features editor at *Suburban Trends*, a newspaper, and co-editor of *Now Culture*, a literary magazine. He was recently awarded First Place in Arts and Entertainment Writing by the New Jersey Press Association. His poems have been published in *Word Salad, Tight, Graven Images, Candlestones, E-verse Radio,* the *Haiku and Twitter Poems* chapbook by World Class Poetry Blog, *The Rutherford Red Wheelbarrow Anthology,* and *Double Room,* among others.

PAUL NASH is a naturalist and writer whose works have included narrative fiction and poetry as well as scientific and historical articles. He tries to maintain a balance between his scientific studies and his literary endeavors. Paul conducts laboratory and field research on ancient organisms preserved in amber and sedimentary rock at the American Museum of Natural History in New York City. He co-hosts the longstanding North Jersey Literary Series founded by members of The Rift Arts Forum in 1997 and currently held monthly in Teaneck, New Jersey. He is on the board of directors of The Poet's Press and is a fiction editor for *Sensations Magazine*. Paul was senior editor of *The Rift Arts Forum Publication* from 1996 to 1999. One of Paul's short stories has just appeared in the international journal *The Istanbul Literary*

< 157 >

Review (www.ilrmagazine.net) in January 2010; two of his poems were published in *The Rutherford Red Wheelbarrow Anthology* (September 2009). Paul recently participated in two international scientific expeditions to Gujarat, India (January 2009 and 2010), where he and his colleagues excavated 52-million-year-old amber. Paul is currently authoring several scientific papers based on ongoing research. He is past-president of the New York Paleontological Society.

REBECCA PIERSON is a student at the Academy of Art University in San Francisco, pursuing a BFA with emphasis on storyboarding animation. She plans to obtain a Masters in Fine Arts, concentrating on sculpture and oil painting.

MARIANNE POLOSKEY is a widely published poet whose work has appeared in such literary journals as *North American Review, Louisiana Literature, Paterson Literary Review, Connecticut Review, Phi Kappa Phi Forum, Potomac Review, River Oak Review, SLANT, Palo Alto Review, Eclipse, The Spoon River Poetry Review, Phoebe,* and *Visions International*. She has had dozens of her poems published in *The Christian Science Monitor*. Her work is also in several anthologies, including *Inside Grief; Rough Places Plain: Poems of the Mountains; American Diaspora; Red, White & Blues;* and *Stories from Where We Live: The South Atlantic Coast and Piedmont — A Literary Field Guide*. She has written poetry book reviews for *Valparaiso Poetry Review, Red Rock Review, Rattle,* and for www.smartishpace.com. Her first collection is titled *Climbing the Shadows*.

S. GILI POST has roots in the post-punk psychedelic music scene that was centered in NYC's Lower East Side in the 1980s and 1990s. She has written and performed on a number of recordings produced by Music Maniac Records. Since the latter 1990s, Suzanne has lent her voice to poetry and playwriting. She performed off Broadway with other "Rifters" at the Red Room, and continues to stage performances and recitals, and to host poetry readings at venues such as *Wanted — Poets Dead and Alive* and the *Underground Railroad Museum Poetry Salon*, both in Burlington County, New Jersey. Her work has been published recently in *Sensations Magazine, The Haddonfield Anthology,* and online by *The Zen Society*. Suzanne is currently researching and composing

< 158 >

ritual ceremonies for women — paying homage to her Maltese heritage. Along with Suzanne's professional and personal interests in literature and the arts, she now enjoys the meditative transport of simple things like petting zoos and firefly hatchings.

DANIEL P. QUINN directed the U.S. premieres of master British playwright Edward Bond's *Derek* — staged at New York's Lincoln Center — and *Stone*. He co-produced the OBIE award-winning production of *Diary of a Madman* at the Irish Arts Center, where his work also included Graham Reid's *Remembrance* and Janet Noble's *Away Alone*. While at the Park Performing Arts Center, Mr. Quinn produced *The Passion Play* with Eric Hafen, which received national and international attention for the casting of an African American actor in the role of Jesus. During his tenure as artistic director of the New Stagecraft Company, he received a proclamation from the Manhattan Borough President for the company's award-winning and challenging works and world premieres. In 2000, Mr. Quinn was invited by New York's Department of French Cultural Services to establish a cultural exchange between Lyons and its sister city, Paterson, New Jersey. Mr. Quinn was also a guest of Aer Lingus at the Dublin Theatre Festival in Ireland. He was invited by Claudio Abbado to be a directing assistant at the Teatro alla Scala in Milan, Italy. Mr. Quinn is a member of the Society of Stage Directors and Choreographers, and he is the author of *Exits and Entrances: Producing Off-Broadway, Opera & Beyond: 1981-2006* (2007) and *Organized Labor* (2004), a poetry collection.

JAMIE MCNEELY QUIRK writes, edits, and knits near Princeton, New Jersey, where she works at both a private school and a public library. Her poems have appeared in *The Macguffin, Journal of New Jersey Poets,* and *The Lyric,* among other places. For four years (1999-2003) she hosted a monthly open mic series in Paramus and led workshops through various adult education programs in northern New Jersey. Having earned an MFA from Sarah Lawrence College, she is currently pursuing a Masters degree in Library and Information Science at Rutgers University.

< 159 >

SUSANNA RICH is a 2009 Emmy Award nominee for poetry she wrote and voice-overed for Craig Lindvahl's documentary *Cobb Field: A Day at the Ballpark*. She is the author of two poetry chapbooks, *Television Daddy* and *The Drive Home* (both from Finishing Line Press). Susanna was the 2008 Featured Poet of *Darkling Literary Magazine*. She is a Fulbright Fellow in Creative Writing, Collegium Budapest Fellow, and Pushcart Prize nominee. An internationally published poet and prose writer with hundreds of credits, Susanna is currently touring her "one-woman audience-interactive poetry experiences": *Television Daddy* and *The Drive Home*. Her work has appeared in such journals as *The Evansville Review, Feminist Studies, Nimrod, Phoebe* (both Fairfax and Oneonta), *English Journal, Pilvax* (Budapest), *Porcupine, Southern California Review, Sensations Magazine, Tiferet, Urthona* (UK), *Willow Review, LIPS,* and *Zone* 3. She is Professor of English and Distinguished Teacher at Kean University in New Jersey, where she teaches courses on Emily Dickinson, William Blake, and twentieth-century women poets. Please visit her at www.susannarich.com.

EDDIE RIVERA was born and raised in Paterson, New Jersey. He started writing at the age of 20, and has published a chapbook, *My Sentiments Exactly* (1996). Eddie was a member of POET-X, a five-person poetry performance group that was initiated in 1997 and active for several years. He and the other four members of the group all appear in this anthology. He has been a featured poet in many New Jersey venues, including the *North Jersey Literary Series* (Teaneck, New Jersey), the Rochelle Park Library poetry series, Borders (Wayne and Paramus, New Jersey), and the Specialty Cup (Ridgewood, New Jersey). His poetry has appeared in *Sensations Magazine* and *The Rift Arts Forum Publication*. In 2002, Eddie was also one of 11 poets who performed in John Salacan's *The Muse Pool*, a multimedia theatrical production of music and poetry. Eddie has been involved in graphic arts his whole life, and he was technical assistant on Daniel P. Quinn's book, *Exits and Entrances*. His reading tastes are primarily in Greek literature, Shakespeare, and fantasy/science fiction. You can find a poem about Eddie's long-lived-in Paterson apartment in Brett Rutherford's book, *Whippoorwill Road: The Supernatural Poems*. Recently, Eddie became a father to a baby boy.

< 160 >

DENISE RUE has been published in *Poet Lore, Paterson Literary Review, Inkwell, Alimentum,* and *Miller's Pond,* among other literary journals. She received her MFA in poetry from Sarah Lawrence College in 2003 and has taught poetry in schools, nursing homes, and a women's prison. She is a two-time finalist in the Allen Ginsberg Poetry Contest and was the 2005 Judson Jerome Poetry Scholarship recipient, which enabled her to attend the Antioch Writer's Conference. She works as a clinical hypnotherapist and as a hospice volunteer.

C. D. RUSSELL's work has been published in several scientific journals as well as *The Handbook of Obesity* and *The Panhandler.* She lives in the rurals of New Jersey with a poet husband and a champagne schnoodle.

BRETT RUTHERFORD is a poet, novelist, and playwright, with a focus on the Gothic and neo-Romantic. He has lived and worked in Weehawken, New Jersey; New York City; and Providence, Rhode Island. During his Manhattan years, he founded The Poet's Press to promote the work of lesser-known but deserving poets. The press is active in print and online, with close to 200 publications to date (www.poetspress.org). His play *Night Gaunts,* about horror writer H. P. Lovecraft, was broadcast as a radio drama in Boston in 2005, and then staged in Heidelberg, Germany, in 2006. His verse play, *Carlota, Empress of Mexico,* was given a staged reading by The Writers' Circle of Providence in the summer of 2007. His most recent books of poetry are *Things Seen in Graveyards* (2007), *Doctor Jones and Other Terrors* (2008) and *Twilight of the Dictators* (2009). During a "back to school" adventure, he completed his Master's degree in English at the University of Rhode Island in 2007. He works for the university in distance learning and teaches literature in the Women's Studies Department.

JOHN SALACAN was actively involved in the "Palisades," or "Hudson River," poetry scene during the 1990s and early 2000s. His poems have appeared in such magazines as *The Ever Dancing Muse, The Rift,* and *Sensations.* He has two poetry collections, *Season of Saxophones and Sea Nymphs* and *Conversations with the Corn God.* He is also an artist and has had many of his illustrations and cartoons published. For the last 35 years, John has been a musical composer, writing art songs,

< 161 >

violin concertos, symphonies, and tone poems. In 1980 he won a grant from the New Jersey State Council on the Arts for his ballet *The Hunt of the Unicorn*. His *Watching Suite* was choreographed and performed by Barbara Sheehey's Park Dance Company in Rahway, New Jersey. In 2002 he staged a multimedia theatrical production of music and poetry entitled *The Muse Pool*, featuring 11 poets who appear in this anthology. John also wrote most of the music for this performance. In 2006, he moved to the Nevada desert with his wife, Aysa, and is currently a book conservator, binder, and publisher.

JOSEPH ANDREW SAPIA was a member of the poetry performance group POET-X and an active participant in the Palisades Poetry Movement of the late 1990s. His work has been published in the *Paterson Literary Review*, the Ocean County Artist Guild's annual journal *Coffeehouse Poems*, *The Rift*, and *Sensations Magazine*. He staged events through the Black Box Theater in Asbury Park, New Jersey — this organization sponsored his Beat Generation spoof reading, known as "The Beat Off," which took place annually between 2000 and 2004. Sapia has appeared as a featured poet at numerous venues in the tristate area. He is also the author of the 2002 book *The Complete Guide to Lost Pet Prevention and Recovery*, co-authored with Patricia Sapia, published by El Jebel Press.

S. THOMAS SUMMERS is a teacher of literature and writing in northern New Jersey, at both Wayne Hills High School and Passaic County Community College (in Wanaque). He is the author of two chapbooks: *Death Settled Well* (Shadows Ink Publications, 2006) and *Rather, It Should Shine* (Pudding House Press, 2007). His work has appeared in *Umbrella*, *Triggerfish*, *Pedestal Magazine*, *The Oak Bend Review*, and other print and electronic journals. His poem, "A Fall from Grace," was recently named the InterBoard Poetry Community poem of the year. Some of Mr. Summers' work can be read online at www.thelintinmypocket.wordpress.com.

JOHN J. TRAUSE is director of the Oradell Public Library, and past director of the Wood-Ridge Memorial Library (both in New Jersey). He has two chapbooks: *Seriously Serial* (Poets Wear Prada, 2007), and *Latter-Day Litany* (Éditions élastiques, 1996). In 2009 John was nomi-

< 162 >

nated for a Pushcart Prize. His translations, poetry and visual work appear or are forthcoming in numerous publications, including *Sensations Magazine, Cover, The Rift, Xavier Review, The Alternative News, Radix, Now Culture, The Rutherford Red Wheelbarrow Anthology, The Journal of New Jersey Poets, Lips, Offerta Speciale, Plainsongs, Brevitas,* and *Sulphur River Review,* among others, and in online journals like *Sidereality, Pedestal Magazine,* and *ditch.* His work has also appeared in the artists' periodical *Crossings* (Brooklyn Waterfront Artists Coalition). *Latter-Day Litany & Other Pseudo-Hagiographica* (the stage version of his chapbook) has been produced off-off Broadway and elsewhere by Daniel P. Quinn since 1998. In both 2005 and 2006, he was chosen along with Jerome Rothenberg to participate in the Visible Word exhibition and poetry reading (Stevens Institute, Hoboken, New Jersey), which paired poets and visual artists. In 2005 he co-founded the William Carlos Williams Poetry Cooperative in Rutherford, New Jersey, where he serves as programmer and host. For the sake of art, Mr. Trause hung naked for one whole month in the summer of 2007 on the Art Wall of the Bowery Poetry Club. At various times in his life he has been mistaken for being a priest, a policeman, a pimp, and a pornographer. He is none of these.

DORIS UMBERS is the founder and editor of *Bluestone Quarry Press,* a broadside publication; she was managing editor of *Etruscan Press* from 2008 to 2010, the editor of *Harpur Palate* from 2003 to 2005, and a copy editor for *Global Scholarly Publications* from 2002 to 2004. Her work has appeared in various literary journals, notably in *Columbia: A Journal of Literature and Art, Green Mountains Review,* and the *Paterson Literary Review.* Her poetry has won numerous awards, including finalist in the John Ciardi Prize for Poetry First Book Award (2009), semifinalist in the Crab Orchard Series in Poetry First Book Award (2009), finalist for the Carolyn Kizer Prize in Poetry (2006), second place in the Allen Ginsberg Poetry Award (2005), and winner of the Academy of American Poets University Prize (2003 and 2004), among others. She has a PhD in English and teaches at Empire State College, New York.

GALEN WARDEN is both poet and artist. She was raised on a slim budget by a single mother who was active in the civil rights movement of the 1960s. She spent vacations with her father in the Connecticut

< 163 >

suburbs — complete with yacht clubs and sailing trips. This dual citizenship of privilege and humble means provided Galen with a rare opportunity to develop an informed opinion of the world and her place in it. She has been both an artist and a poet all of her life. From the bonfires of adolescence through the maze of raising six children, and now into the soaring flights of real grown-up adventures, poetry has been a constant vehicle for catharsis, communication, and celebration. Galen has been honored to be published internationally, nationally, and locally in various anthologies, literary magazines, and journals, including *Sensations Magazine, Lips, The Paterson Literary Review, The Ever Dancing Muse, The Book of Hope, The World Book of Healing,* and most recently *Get Satisfied: How 20 People Like You Found the Satisfaction of Enough.* She has also appeared in several small chapbooks, both hers and others'— her latest book, *Invoking Eros,* is a collection of erotic and semi-erotic poems and paintings. Galen resides in Rockaway, New Jersey, and at the time of this publication, is a marketing manager for LexisNexis.

DONALD ZIRILLI was born on an island. He is the editor of *Now Culture.* His poetry has been published by *Art Times, Iota, Anti-, Specs Journal,* and *River Styx,* among other places.

< 164 >

CITATIONS

"Mullican Pines" appeared in *Sensations Magazine* Issue #20: "Scenic New Jersey" (2000).

"Amtraked" appeared in *Sensations Magazine* Issue #37 (2004/2005).

"García's House" and "pomegranate" are from an unpublished collection entitled *Forbidden Fruit.*

"Time" appeared in *Sensations Magazine* Issue #32 (2003).

"Like—Dust" appeared in *The Rift Arts Forum Publication,* "Evolving" Issue (1998).

"Slipstream" appeared in *Sensations Magazine* Issue #42: "Spoken Word" (2007), and was later revised for this anthology.

"Curves" appeared in special issue #17 of *River Oak Review*: "In Memoria" (September 2001).

"Nun Flying Through Walls" appeared in the online journal *Literary Bohemian* [2010].

"Cigarettes, Coffee, and Beer, Oh Dear" appeared in the online publication *ditch* [Saturday, August 22, 2009].

"The Absence of Crows" appeared in *The Paterson Literary Review* Issue #34 (2004).

"When I Was Electrocuted" appeared in *The Paterson Literary Review* Issue #26 (1997).

"The Cross-Dressers of Antietam" appeared in *Sensations Magazine* Issue #46: '19th Century America' (2009), and will appear in Mr. Messineo's seventh poetry book, *Historiopticon.*

< 165 >

"Mr. Lee Eats an Apple, April 1865" is part of an unpublished collection entitled *Forbidden Fruit*.

"It Is a Sin" appeared in *Sensations Magazine* Issue #40: "Retro" (2006).

"Against Their Will" appeared in *WLA - War Literature & the Arts: Journal of the Humanities*, Vol. 17, #1 & 2 (2005).

"Origami" appeared in Ms. Warden's poetry collection: *Invoking Eros*, expanded edition (2008).

"She Walks Softly" was published in George C. Harvilla's chapbook *Big Bang Gumbo* (1997).

"Utility" appeared in *Four Walls* (1994).

"Parasitoid" appeared in *The Rift Arts Forum Publication*, 'Surfacing' Issue (1996).

"The Harvestman" appeared in Brett Rutherford's collection entitled *Things Seen in Graveyards*.

"Dreams" is a new and previously unpublished poem, written for the occasion of this anthology. Mr. Messineo wanted to explore the relationship between discoverers/promoters of talent and the 'discovered/promoted', and how that can change over time. Though partly inspired by personal experience, and titled after the theme issue of *The Rift Arts Forum Publication* that was never finished nor released, it is neither reflective of any one incident with any one individual "and is not reflective of my relationship with The Rift Arts Forum, which I enjoyed during its years of activity."

"The Watcher" appeared in Brett Rutherford's book *The Gods As They Are, On Their Planets* (2005).

< 166 >

ART CREDITS

Cover art: Roy Lucianna, *River View from Edgewater* (1989). Wood cut, 6" x 8"

Title-page and section-title pages: Roy Lucianna, *Apollonian Sun Self* (2000). Sealing wax, deerskin, sawblade, 10" diam.

Page 14: Tom Fitzpatrick, *The First Four* (1988). Ink drawing on illustration board.

Page 89: Rebecca Pierson, *Portrait of Grandfather* (2006). Charcoal.

Pages 131-132: Galen Warden, Pencil drawings.

Typography, cover design and book design: Brett Rutherford.

< 167 >

www.ingramcontent.com/pod-product-compliance
Lightning Source LLC
Chambersburg PA
CBHW031133090426
42738CB00008B/1071